40-DAY REVOLUTION

A STRATEGY TO IMPACT YOUR WORLD FOR CHRIST

Operation Light Force is an international Christian organization. It is our mission to grow biblical disciples, and to bring about in their lives personal and **global spiritual transformation.** We envision the transformation of an entire generation of believers who have grown to **think, act and be like Jesus –** for their entire lives.

ISBN 978-0-9814923-5-3

Cover and Interior Design by Jeff Damm Design

Some of the anecdotal illustrations in this book are true accounts of actual events, and are included with the permission of the persons involved. All other illustrations are composites of real situations, and any resemblance to people living or dead is coincidental.

Unless otherwise identified, all Scripture quotations in this publication are taken from the HOLY BIBLE: NEW INTERNATIONAL VERSION® (NIV®). Copyright © 1973, 1978, 1984 by International Bible Society. Used by permission of Zondervan Publishing House. All rights reserved. Other versions used (and so noted) include: Contemporary English Version (CEV). © 1992 by American Bible Society and King James Version (KJV).

Mull, Richard, 1964-Present
Mull, Andrew, 1993-Present

40-Day Revolution : a strategy to impact your world for Christ / Richard & Andrew Mull.
ISBN 978-0-9814923-5-3
1. Students–Religious life. 2. Evangelistic work. I. Title: Forty day revolution. II. Title.

OPERATION LIGHT FORCE
2310 Leonard Drive
Seffner, FL 33584
www.operationlightforce.com
www.40dayrevolution.com
813.657.6147 phone

Revolution!

The word revolution itself stands for radical change. Revolutions change lives. Revolutions change nations. Revolutions have changed history. Revolutions can change the future.

Revolutions are always preceded by a growing awareness that things are not the way they ought to be. It has become obvious that there is a great need for change on the campuses of America. Some feel that answers do not exist. But an answer does exist.

It Is Time for a Revolution!

Revolutions are not glamorous. They are not for the weak. Every revolution is the product of a generation whose motto is "No Fear." It is our challenge to **BE** such a generation

Our weapons are not guns, knives, or bombs, but rather something much more powerful. Campuses are being revolutionized through the power of God's love, as it is manifested through prayer, blessing, and serving others in the lives of a "Revival Generation."

When Babylon's laws conflicted with Daniel's faith, he chose, rather than to disobey God, to pray, and face the consequences.

Will you bring prayer back to your school? Will you be a part of The Revolution?

"—we must fight!—I repeat it, Sirs, we must fight!! "...They tell us, sirs, that we are weak—unable to cope with so formidable an adversary ...Sir we are not weak, if we make a proper use of those means which the God of nature hath placed in our power ...Besides, Sir, we shall not fight our battles alone. There is a God who presides over the destinies of nations and who will raise up friends to fight our battles for us. The battle, Sir, is not to the strong alone; it is to the vigilant, the active, the brave.

"...Gentlemen may cry, peace, peace—but there is no peace. The war is actually begun! Is life so dear or peace so sweet to be purchased at the price of chains and slavery? Forbid it, Almighty God!—I know not what course others may take; but as for me, ...give me liberty, or give me death!"

—PATRICK HENRY, LEADER IN THE AMERICAN REVOLUTION,
FROM "THE INEVITABLE WAR" SPEECH MARCH, 1775.

[PREPARE FOR REVOLUTION]

You are joining tens of thousands of Christian students worldwide who are participating in **OPERATION LIGHT FORCE'S 40-Day Campaign** to live out the Christian life on middle school, high school, and college campuses.

How Is This Campaign Unique?

There are three strategic elements to the 40-Day Revolution:

1. FASTING AND PRAYER

Choosing to sacrifice something we enjoy helps us to focus our attention on God, transforms us, and prepares us to hear God's voice.

Fasting moves the heart of God because it is a work of faith. Fasting is also an act of humility. Fasting and prayer get us ready, so that God can answer prayers through us.

Our prayers and fasting can be the instruments to transform our campuses. Even Jesus' disciples discovered that sometimes evil is only removed from a place through prayer and fasting.

2. SERVANTHOOD AND BLESSING

"The 40-Day Revolution" explains, in clear terms, biblical principles that can be easily integrated into a lifestyle.

Believers and nonbelievers agree that positive, ethical, and moral lifestyles are needed to save this world from self-destruction.

3. DAILY PRAYER IN SCHOOL

Until June 25, 1962, students in many of the public schools of America held daily times of prayer. On that fateful day, the US Supreme court ruled that officially sanctioned prayer – regardless of the content – in public schools constituted an unconstitutional endorsement of religion.

Since that time, every facet of life on the American campus has been severely impacted. The greatest behavioral problems of that time – gum chewing and talking in class – have been replaced by sexual promiscuity, drugs, alcohol, violence, racism, bullying, and a host of other offenses.

It is time for a revolution of prayer. It's unlikely that legislation will bring prayer back into our schools. It is up to this generation to pray daily for their campuses and for a revival in their schools.

[WHY 40 DAYS]

The objective of the 40-Day Campaign is to create a heart for God in the life of each participant. Godly habits are established by living for God one day at a time. **Forty days of sacrifice** – one day at a time – leads to a 40-day habit of service, a solid foundation for a lifestyle of selfless love!

It takes twenty-one days to form a habit.

A pastor in California was walking on the beach one morning, when he suddenly found himself in the midst of a swarm of flies. Never in all of his walks on the beach had he been under such a barrage of pesky flies.

As he thought about the flies, the Holy Spirit asked him, "What are the names of Satan?" He pondered the names from Scripture: liar, father of lies, destroyer, and roaring lion. Then it struck him…… Beelzebub is one of the names of Satan, and it means "lord of the flies."

The pastor went home and began to study flies. He soon found that the life cycle of a fly is typically 40 days. Therefore, 40 days of sustained treatment is needed to wipe out an infestation of flies.

In citrus growing areas, such as Florida, there is a fly called the Mediterranean fruit fly, which can cause major problems, resulting in great destruction of citrus crops.

When an infestation of this fly occurs, it is as if everyone is living in a battle-zone. The state declares war on this tiny creature and carries out prolonged aerial and ground assaults. A one-time spraying is useless. It takes 40 days to wipe out a complete life cycle.

Why so much talk about flies? It is time to go beyond the tradition of onetime Christian events. If we want to defeat the "lord of the flies," Satan, we must begin prolonged spiritual assaults. The 40-Day Campaign is a sustained treatment of Godly influence against Satan's destructive strategy on our campuses.

Do you need more information? Want to know more about doing an assignment? Want to know how someone else did an assignment for a day? Visit our web site at www. operationlightforce.com.

Share your creativity and experiences. Post your story and picture; we may put your testimony in our newsletter.

[WHY SHOULD I FAST?]

Fasting is a sacrifice. You first need to ask God what you should fast. What one thing, if you gave up it for a time, would draw you closer to God?

Fasting Changes Nations.

Throughout history when a nation or a group of people sought God with fasting and prayer, God moved in powerful ways. It is accurate to say that fasting literally changed the course of entire nations. Esther, from the Old Testament, was only a youth when she called the Jews to fast, and it changed the world.

The first thought of some people is, "What is the least that I can fast to get by?" Such an attitude expresses a shallowness of love for God. Express your love for God with a **serious** sacrifice.

> "Fasting begets prophets and strengthens strong men. Fasting makes lawgivers wise; it is the soul's safeguard, the body's trusted comrade, the armor of the champion, the training of the athlete."
>
> —Basil, Bishop of Caesarea (A.D. 330 - 379).

With the call to enter into extended fasts, we must prepare ourselves adequately so that the fast can honor God and fulfill its purpose. The following information is provided to help and encourage you.

1. ***Ask God what He would have you to fast.*** We encourage you to incorporate a FOOD ELEMENT to your fast and a MEDIA COMPONENT.

> 🐟 In terms of a FOOD ELEMENT, some have fasted lunch every day, some have fasted their favorite soda, sweets and some have done a Daniel fast that, simply put, means to not eat sweets or meat.

> 🐟 And, in terms of a MEDIA COMPONENT, it is important to examine your life and ask God if there are any areas of media, or all, that have consumed your life more than God. Yeah, I thought so! It is just 40-days and you will survive. Some have cut out all media, some have fasted their favorite TV show. Again, ask God and fast something that will be a sacrifice.

2. ***If you believe God wants you to do a substantial fasting of food, seek medical advice and permission before beginning the fast.*** Seek medical advice before an significant food fast, especially if you have any existing medical concerns or conditions. If you are under eighteen years of age, discuss your desire to fast with your parents.

Spiritual covering, submission, and unity are important factors when fasting. Discuss your plans with your youth leader and/or church leaders. Remember, fasting is an attitude of the heart! Ask them if they would consider fasting with you!

3. ***Fast and pray in order to humble yourself and purify your worship***. In fasting we are not trying to get something from God, but rather seeking to realign our hearts' affections with His.

In fasting we can more readily say, "We love you, Lord, more than anything in the world." Lust of any kind is a perverted form of worship, but fasting enables us to cleanse the sanctuary of our hearts from every other rival.

4. ***Don't boast about your fast***. But—let people know you won't be eating, if you need to (Matthew 6:16-18).

5. ***Do the fast with someone else.*** Two are better than one! We encourage parents and children to consider fasting together. Several generations fasting together have a powerful impact!

6. ***Have a clear target for prayer focus.*** Without a vision (a clear prayer goal) the people perish.

During a fast, I have four or five prayer goals that are clearly articulated. When I'm not deeply motivated by a clear goal, I usually fast until breakfast!

When God shows you something, write down your vision, so you can run with it (Habukkuk 2:2).

7. ***Make your commitment.*** It can be very helpful to choose more than one item to fast. We strongly encourage you to fast everything that pulls you down spiritually. Fast something that will increase your prayer life.

Biblical fasts always consisted of food. Therefore, we encourage you to seriously consider one of the following fasts:

- A Daniel fast, with vegetables and water, is good for those carrying a heavy work load (like moms and students). Fasting "meats and sweets" can be done by athletes who can get protein from other food sources.

- A fruit or vegetable juice fast allows you to enter into fasting, but still provides enough energy to function. Many people have done a 40-day juice fast. Out of consideration for their health and metabolism, I would encourage teenagers to use juice and protein drinks for sustenance. If you have sugar sensitivities or problems, consult your physician before attempting a liquid fast.

- A water only fast has been done by many people. ***We would not encourage a water fast without strong medical supervision, <u>particularly for youth.</u>*** A water only fast is very difficult, but very effective. Depending on your weight and metabolism, you can go 40 days on water alone.

- A total fast is without water. ***Do-Not-ever-go beyond three days without water!*** Discuss your plans with your doctor, youth leader and/or church leaders, and parents. ***We do not encourage this type of fast without specific confirmation from the Lord through your parents and church leadership.***

8. *Make time to pray and read the Word*. Praying and reading God's Word may seem obvious, but busyness and distractions can keep you from devotions. Reading books with testimonies of victories gained through fasting will encourage you, for example: Changing History through Prayer and Fasting by Derek Prince, Fast Forward by Lou Engle, and God's Chosen Fast by Author Wallis.

9. *Expect to hear God's voice in the Word, dreams, visions and revelations.* Daniel prepared himself to receive revelation through fasting (Daniel 10:1,2). There is a fasting reward (Matthew 6:18).

A Malaysian brother shared that during a 40-day fast he was "caught up into the heavens." After the fast, he took a team into the interior of Borneo and saw a dead woman raised, causing revival to break out in her village.

10. *Prepare for opposition.* On the day of your fast, you can bet doughnuts will be at the office or in class. Your spouse (or your mom) will suddenly be inspired to cook your favorite meals. ***Press through!***

Many times you may feel more tension build at home. My fasts are just as difficult for my wife as they are for me. Satan tempted Jesus during the fast, and we must expect the same. Discouragement may come in like a flood, but recognize the source and take your stand on the victory of Christ.

11. *If you fail, don't give in to condemnation.* The "to fast or not to fast" dilemma can be a major tool of the enemy. Even though you may fail several times, God always extends grace.

Once, I gave up on a fast and sneaked some yogurt and chips. The next day an intercessor came to me and said, "I saw you in a dream. You were supposed to be fasting, but you were eating yogurt and chips." It was pretty good motivation to start again!

12. *Feel free to rest a lot,* and continue to exercise, with supervision.

13. *Breakthroughs often come <u>after a fast</u>, not during it.* Do not listen to the lie that nothing is happening. It is my conviction that every fast done in faith will be rewarded.

14. *Break the fast slowly, over several days, with fruit juice or light soups.* During a light juice fast or a water fast your digestive system shuts down. Eating too much too soon can be dangerous. Break the fast with several days of diluted, non-acidic juice, then regular juice, followed by fruits and vegetables.

May thousands of young men and women fast as God leads them. May they find a greater intimacy with God the Father. May they be used in the greatest revival we have ever seen.

> *Let two generations arise and fulfill this divine mandate! We have taught our children how to feast and play. Now it is time to teach them how to fast and pray!*
> *– Lou Engle*

[SOCIAL MEDIA REVOLUTION]

Social media has become a primary means of communication for our generation. In itself social media is neither good, nor evil. Unfortunately, it has often been used in ways that are not pleasing to God and often in ways that are down-right evil. It is time for a **Holy Revolution** in our lives concerning social media.

Cyber-bullying has become an epidemic that has deeply wounded many people. It has even led to an increase in suicides. Sexting has ruined the reputations of many, brought on shame, and been a gateway to more illicit behaviors. With God's help we can redeem social media.

The process begins with understanding the power of words; the power of what we speak, text, forward, and write in any and all forms. We have the power to bring hope, encouragement, and life; and to lead people closer to God. Our words also have the power to hurt, discourage, create heartache, and worse. Posts that include images are viewed more quickly and by more eyes than posts without images, because "A picture is worth a thousand words".

Will you commit your social media to God for the next 40-Days? We offer suggestions every day for the next 40-Days for ways to include your social media as a platform for bringing a revolution to your school.

Imagine hundreds, thousands and tens of thousands of your peers posting every day for 40-Days—images, words that encourage people, cause people to look to God, and even cause a transformation at your school, youth group and city.

Even if you are fasting social media, pray about fasting everything except the use of social media to encourage, witness, and reflect Christ.

You can use our suggestions or come up with a myriad of other creative ways to show the love of Christ. Share your memes with us, share your ideas with us on the www.40DayRevolution.com website.

FRIENDSHIP OR BLESSING EVANGELISM

When you bless a person and are used by God to bring that person closer to God, you are practicing **blessing evangelism**. It is relational, rather than instructional. You share yourself, your time and your heart, rather than your knowledge of how to become a Christian. By sharing in this way in the present, you establish the right to share the wonderful message of Jesus in the future.

> *Key Verse: Proverbs 18:21* "The tongue has the power of life and death."
>
> *James 3:9-10* "With the tongue we praise our Lord and Father, and with it we curse men, who have been made in God's likeness. Out of the same mouth come praise and cursing. My brothers, this should not be."

By our words we can turn people away from God, or we can make people thirsty for God. Even Scripture, which should impart life, can be used to wound as well as to heal. Blessing evangelism occurs when we see people as they have been made in the image of God—we see God's potential in a person, and we strive to bring it out.

Jesus spent time with people, and saw in them the image of God. In many biblical accounts Jesus spent time and blessed people who were normally shunned and considered outcasts.

A story is told of a teacher who had extra time one day and gave her class the assignment of writing something positive about each student in the room. She gathered the students' papers, and for each student she compiled a list of encouraging words written about him or her.

Years later when she would meet any of these students, they would show her the wrinkled old note they had clung to all their lives. One of her students was killed in a war, and in his pocket was found the note that he'd carried since that day.

Here are several ways to bless a person:

- Spend time with them, as Jesus did
- Speak encouraging words
- Listen
- Share
- Write a note

[SERVANT EVANGELISM]

Servant evangelism really is faith in action. In servant evangelism, we seek to meet the needs of those around us. People are needy. By meeting a person's need, we hope to earn the right to share Jesus with them.

>   *Key Verse: John 13:14-15* "Now that I, your Lord and Teacher, have washed your feet, you also should wash one another's feet. I have set you an example that you should do as I have done for you."

In Jesus' day, washing feet was a practical act of service, since they walked barefoot or in sandals wherever they went. The distasteful job was normally the responsibility of the lowliest of the household servants. Jesus taught servanthood when He, the King of Kings, washed the feet of His disciples.

How can you be a servant to a fellow student? It may not go over very well to bring a bucket of water to school and offer to wash people's feet. There is a place for that, but the cafeteria is probably not the place!

You could pick up a student's trash or tray at lunch. You could help him or her get to the car when he or she is struggling with a pile of books and the sky looks gray. Look for practical things that someone has to do.

When you see an opportunity to help, ask yourself, "Why not me? Why not now?" Consider ways to serve your teachers, family, friends, and people in church.

When you serve other people, you break through their defenses.

>   *Romans 12:20-21* states, "On the contrary: If your enemy is hungry, feed him; if he is thirsty, give him something to drink. In doing this, you will heap burning coals on his head. Do not be overcome by evil, but overcome evil with good." We can overcome evil done to us by deeds of kindness rather than seeking revenge.

During the next 40 days, you will be asked to serve people in a variety of ways. You don't have to say anything when you serve them. They may ask you why you are serving them – or they may not.

Many times you may have a chance to explain to them what you are doing. You can tell them that you want to be more like your hero, Jesus, the ultimate servant!

[PRAYER EVANGELISM]

"Talk to God about your friends before talking to your friends about God." — ED SILVOSO

Key Verse: II Corinthians 10:4-5, KJV *"For the weapons of our warfare are not carnal, but mighty through God to the pulling down of strong holds; casting down imaginations, and every high thing that exalteth itself against the knowledge of God, and bringing into captivity every thought to the obedience of Christ."*

Also, **II Chronicles 7:14** *"If my people, who are called by my name, will humble themselves and pray and seek my face and turn from their wicked ways, then will I hear from heaven and will forgive their sin and will heal their land."* And it is completely in keeping with the spirit of that promise to add, *"their campus, home, city or nation"!*

Prayer is our most powerful weapon! Prayer is essential in our lives as well as in the life of our church. It is the power that transforms lives. Without prayer, there is no power.

If you want to be a positive influence on your campus, you must take prayer seriously. We must humbly approach God, and pour out our hearts to Him on behalf of our schools. Prayer, like nothing else, has the power to change a person, club, youth group, school, city, state, nation, and ultimately, the world.

If you are not bold enough to talk to others, but you spend more time in prayer, you may have more influence and power than the one who talks boldly, but with little prayer and no power.

Pray privately to receive God's power. Pray with a friend. Pray as a group. Pray silently. Pray aloud. Read a prayer from the Bible. Pray from your heart as you would speak to a friend. Just pray! Do it often and with a heart for God. Pray that He will change you first, and that He will then change others through you.

Students have prayed with wonderful results. They have seen people healed, marriages restored, lives saved, and their campuses turned right-side-up for God.

We have said a lot about prayer, and will be saying more. We should take the time to discuss this activity, to assure that we understand one another.

Everyone who has visited a church has probably heard a leader lead in prayer. Many times, public prayer is offered boldly, in a clear and authoritative voice. The language and the concepts expressed often sound as if the entire prayer came right out of the King James Bible.

You may not feel that you are qualified to pray like that. If that's how you feel about prayer, you may be surprised when we tell you that *"THAT'S A **GOOD** THING!".*

Please take a few minutes to carefully read **Luke 18:10-14**

Notice that the Pharisee (religious leader) sounded very theological, and his prayer was lengthy. In contrast, the tax collector (who would have been a social outcast of that day) prayed just seven simple words. In the NIV, his entire prayer is quoted as, *"God have mercy on me, a sinner."* The Lord Jesus commented that he went home justified, "rather than the other".

Our point? Talk to the Lord in plain language, just as you would talk with a friend. He isn't impressed with theological language—He just wants to hear the thoughts and feelings of your heart. He isn't impressed with a massive "word count" either. Get to the point, tell Him what's on your mind, thank Him that He's already dealing with it, and move on.

We should also point out that you should **NEVER** think that you can or should take authority over God, or demand/command Him to do anything. Bring your requests to Him with deep respect though, and He is eager to hear your prayer.

While we are on the subject of "how to pray", you should know that you can pray any time, any place, in any position, and you don't have to make a sound. God knows your thoughts and feelings. When audible prayers are not appropriate, God understands. Think the words of your prayer – He will hear and accept your prayer just as surely as if it was spoken aloud.

There ARE some basic instructions about praying – when you have the time. In an emergency, the phrase "God help me!" may be all that you have time for, and He will accept that as a complete prayer. Still, we are commanded to pray "In the name of Jesus."

Not only are we assured that God wants to hear our prayers, but we are assured that He will grant our requests. If you need more assurance that God hears your prayer, study **1 John 5:14-15.**

Pray! Pray! Pray!

Expect Miracles!

Expect a great God to do great things – through you!

[A FEW TESTIMONIES]

"Hello . . . I'm Catherine Roberson from Cashiers United Methodist Church in North Carolina. This past weekend Richard Mull presented the 40-Day Revolution to our community youth group at Camp Awanita in Marietta, SC.

I wasn't sure if the kids were "getting it" and what they were thinking until Monday morning. Several kids showed up for the first prayer meeting and have been sharing about the retreat and the revolution – more than I could have imagined! God is already working wonders in our community through these kids, even in the past two days!

So, this leads me to my question . . . the retreat kids' excitement is spreading to their friends who weren't on the retreat, and now many more kids are wanting to join the 40-Day Revolution. Should I buy more packets now and let these kids join in, or ask them to wait until we've gone through this once and plan to do it again in January with the rest of them?

I also don't know if there should be a certain criteria before a child can start it . . . like be a Christian, understand the gospel, go to church, or is it just come one, come all?

I understand their excitement and wanting to be a part of the movement, but some of this calls for a deep commitment, not just "fun and games", candy, bracelets, etc.

I would really like your advice by e-mail; I have dozens of kids pushing me to know if they can join, so please advise me ASAP. Thank you, thank you, thank you! To God be the Glory!"

—CATHERINE, CASHIERS, NORTH CAROLINA

"My name is Abby Dichaus, and I am a member of the youth group at Northeast Presbyterian Church of St. Petersburg, Florida. I am twelve years old, and I am fired up for God because, tonight, we started the first night of The 40-Day Revolution.

It was awesome to see people praising God and glorifying His Name. I just want to thank you for this because, if Operation Light Force was never here, hundreds of people wouldn't have gotten saved. So I thank you, and I encourage you to keep up your work."

—ABBY DICHAUS FROM ST. PETERSBURG, FLORIDA

"I got this new desire for my friends to be saved, and God really brought a holy conviction upon my life. God has given me a burden and a new hope to see my friends saved.

I know that God has honored our fasting and praying, and that He is just waiting to rain down revival on my school, this nation, and the nations of the world."

—JORDAN FROM KANSAS CITY, MISSOURI

[LEADING A FRIEND TO CHRIST]

Leading a friend to Christ doesn't have to be hard! You may refer to these pages, but we encourage you to memorize the key steps; believe, repent, confess your sins, and confess Jesus publicly. Be sure to memorize the scriptures, so you can share the verses from memory (without the book).

BELIEVE

Key Verse: Acts 16:31 "They replied, 'believe in the Lord Jesus, and you will be saved—you and your household.'"

"To believe" in this verse means to put your whole trust in Jesus. The Bible says that we must believe that Jesus Christ died to pay the penalty for our sins, that He rose from the dead, and we must be willing to live for Him.

What a person really believes is demonstrated more by what he or she does than by what he or she says. Believing in Jesus means turning your life away from sin and going in God's direction, rather than going your own way. It doesn't mean that you are already perfect, but that you are striving to love God and let Him have control of your life.

REPENT

Key Verse: Luke 13:3 ". . . But unless you repent, you too will all perish."

"To Repent" means: "to turn away from." We have spent most of our lives "doing our own thing" and following our own agendas, often doing things that did not please God. The Bible calls our self-will "sin". "To Repent" means to turn from sin, or to quit following our own agendas, and to choose to follow God's will. We turn away from or give up things that we know displease God, or from anything that He reveals to us. When we turn from sin, we turn to God, and do the things that please Him.

CONFESS YOUR SINS

Key Verse: 1 John 1:9 "If we confess our sins, he is faithful and just and will forgive us our sins and purify us from all unrighteousness."

Confessing sin is more than just saying, "I'm sorry." It is not just being sorry that God doesn't approve of your actions, or being sorry for doing something wrong because you were caught.

Confession means to agree with God's perspective on the matter, agree that what you did was wrong, and that you hate the wrong just as God hates the wrong.

God hates sin, but He still loves the sinner. God delights in forgiving our sins. That's why He sent Jesus to die on the cross for us – to take away our sins. We must recognize our sins and ask for God's forgiveness. What we must to do is ask Jesus into our lives, confess our sins, and receive His forgiveness.

CONFESS JESUS PUBLICLY

Key Verse: Romans 10:9 *"That if you confess with your mouth, 'Jesus is Lord,' and believe in your heart that God raised him from the dead, you will be saved."*

To confess *"Jesus is Lord"* is to make a public declaration that you are a follower of Jesus. Do not be ashamed to tell others that you are a Christian or to follow His example by being baptized.

When you choose to receive Jesus and become a Christian, you need to share this important decision. Tell your friends, your family, and others. Find someone to baptize you. Meet with other believers to pray and encourage one another.

After you share these four main steps and your friend understands them, it may be time to make a decision. Ask him or her, *"Do you want to ask Jesus to come into your life and forgive your sins and save you?"* You may use the sample prayer below to lead him/her through this most important decision.

Dear Jesus, I confess that I have sinned and I believe You died for my sins.

I believe that God raised You from the dead.

I need you to forgive me and cleanse me from my sins.

I am finished with living for me, and I want to live for you.

Please fill me with your Holy Spirit.

Thank you for saving me, for forgiving me, and for cleansing me.

The following is an explanation of the one-verse method—an illustration you can use to share your faith:

John 3:16 *"God so loved the world that he gave his one and only Son, that whosoever believes in him shall not perish but have eternal life."*

[PRAYER REQUEST LIST]

5 or more people for whom I commit to praying for God's work (blessing, healing, salvation, etc.) in their life for the next 40 days.

NAMES:

_____, _____, _____
_____, _____, _____
_____, _____, _____
_____, _____, _____

PRAYER REQUEST

_____
_____
_____
_____
_____
_____
_____
_____
_____

GIANTS

(Day 2 – What are the biggest issues facing your school campus that you will commit to pray for during the next 40-Days)

_____
_____
_____
_____
_____
_____

40 DAY REVOLUTION

A STRATEGY TO IMPACT YOUR WORLD FOR CHRIST

ASSIGNMENTS

Commissioning Day is that special day when you begin the 40-Day campaign. You declare your intent to be a missionary to your **school, home, and work**. You receive a blessing and promise of prayer support from your church family.

COMMISSIONING DAY

Here are some ideas for this very important day.

1. If possible, be commissioned by a pastor or youth pastor at your church in front of the congregation, or alternately at Sunday School or evening worship. Have a prayer partner stand with you. The pastor should ask, and you should answer the following questions:

    A. Will you pray for the unbelieving students in your school?

    B. Will you carry out the 40-day assignments to the best of your ability? (See Colossians 3:23.)

    C. What will you fast that is a sacrifice to you?

    D. Who is praying for you?

2. Next, the pastor can commission you however he chooses.

    Good things to pray for are: Divine Appointments for ministry, Strength, Courage, Faithfulness, and God's Anointing.

3. If a pastor isn't available, then have your parents or other respected adult commission you. Try to make it as public as you can, so you will be accountable!

SOCIAL MEDIA ASSIGNMENT - Letting the world know about what you're about to start, Maybe a picture of the book on instagram or a link to the website on facebook or twitter. Whatever you feel the Lord leading you to do.

A STRATEGY TO IMPACT YOUR WORLD FOR CHRIST

One girl did the revolution all by herself. She went to the principal's office to ask him how she could pray for him. He gruffly asked who had sent her. She replied, "God did." He asked her to shut the door. When the door was closed, he said, "If your God can bring my wife and daughters back to me, I will believe in him and come to your church."

She prayed, God answered, and her principal was in church on Sunday! You can rock your campus alone or with a group. *JUST BELIEVE!*

Luke 9:1-2 "When Jesus had called the Twelve together, he gave them power and authority to drive out all demons and to cure diseases, and he sent them out to preach the kingdom of God and to heal the sick."

Read: **Acts 1:8, Matthew 22:37-38, Matthew 28:19-20**
(Love your neighbor as yourself.)

JOURNAL

PRAYER

WEEK 1 ~ MEMORY VERSE:

Matthew 22:37-39—The Great Commandment

"Jesus replied: 'Love the Lord your God with all your heart and with all your soul and with all your mind [and with all your strength].' This is the first and greatest commandment. And the second is like it"

[ASSIGNMENT] WEEK 1 ~ DAY 2 ~ MONDAY ____/____/____
[TODAY'S DATE]

David faced Goliath and won a mighty battle. In the same way every person and every school has Giants; the things which are the major issue or problem on campus. God is with you to destroy the Giants.

GIANT'S DAY

1. Ask God to show you the biggest problems in your life and on your campus: (Ask your administrators if necessary)

a. Weapons	e. Absences	i. Vandalism
b. Fighting	f. Drugs/Alcohol	j. Sexual sin
c. Tardiness	g. Theft	k. Worldliness
d. Relational strife	h. Personal Sin	l. Other _____

2. Pray for the issues listed above. If you pray with faith you will change the spiritual climate of your school.

3. Find a rock and paint it. Place your rock somewhere on the outer perimeter of your campus or in a place you will see it daily, (such as in your locker). The rock is a symbol of David's victory over Goliath, the giant. It serves as a reminder that your prayers are taking down the giants at your school.

SOCIAL MEDIA ASSIGNMENT - post this verse on Facebook and/or twitter

> *EPHESIANS 6:12 - For we do not wrestle against flesh and blood, but against principalities, against powers, against the rulers of the darkness of this age, against spiritual hosts of wickedness in the heavenly places.*

> *I Samuel 17:45-47 "You come against me with sword and spear and javelin, but I come against you in the name of the Lord Almighty, the God of the armies of Israel, whom you have defied. This day the Lord will hand you over to me, and I'll strike you down and cut off your head. Today . . . the whole world will know that there is a God in Israel. All those gathered here will know that it is not by sword or spear that the Lord saves; for the battle is the Lord's, and he will give all of you into our hands."*

A STRATEGY TO IMPACT YOUR WORLD FOR CHRIST

HOMESCHOOLERS

Homeschoolers may face BIG problems at home, too! They might include distractions, not getting along with siblings, struggling with certain subjects, or even your mom or dad feeling overwhelmed. Ask God to show YOU the specific GIANTS that you face each day. Then, commit to pray daily for these issues.

JOURNAL

What are the Giants on my campus, in my personal life, and in my home?

_____

_____

_____

_____

_____

QUOTE

"Where, oh, where are the eternity-conscious believers? Where are the souls white-hot for God because they fear His holy name and presence and so live with eternity's values in view?" —LEONARD RAVENHILL, REVIVAL GOD'S WAY

PRAYER

_____

_____

_____

_____

_____

_____

_____

WEEK 1 ~ MEMORY VERSE:

Matthew 22:37-39—The Great Commandment

"Jesus replied: 'Love the Lord your God with all your heart and with all your soul and with all your mind [and with all your strength].' This is the first and greatest commandment. And the second is like it"

[ASSIGNMENT]

You have been called to be a light in the darkness. Today you will begin the process of identifying the names and needs of others in each class.

LIGHTHOUSE DAY I - "I PRAY"

Pray for the people seated in front of you, behind you, to your left, and to your right. Write their names and their needs on a desk in the diagram below!

Pray for them. Ask God to show you specific ways to bless, serve, pray for, and tell them of God's love! And also pray that God will orchestrate opportunities to witness to them.

You also have a lighthouse chart that you can use. You will be reminded in the book each week to pray for and be a lighthouse.

To get a lighthouse worksheet from online go to www.40dayrevolution.org

SOCIAL MEDIA ASSIGNMENT - Ask this question on either fb or twitter asking, "What can I Pray for you about?" and then write down what they say, and be sure to pray for them.

> *I Timothy 2:1* *"I urge, then, first of all that requests, prayers, intercession and thanksgiving be made for everyone."*

Prayer Target: Focus upon the needs of 5 or more people.

Document the answers to prayer:

Focus 1: _____

Focus 2: _____

Focus 3: _____

Focus 4: _____

Focus 5: _____

LIGHTHOUSE

1st Period

Your Desk

2nd Period

Your Desk

3rd Period

Your Desk

4th Period

Your Desk

5th Period

Your Desk

6th Period

Your Desk

HOMESCHOOLERS

This is something that you can do, too! Think of the names of youth who live in your neighborhood. Write their names down and any prayer requests that you can think of that they might have. When you've done that, follow the directions above just like everyone else.

JOURNAL

_____

_____

_____

_____

_____

_____

_____

PRAYER

_____

_____

_____

_____

_____

_____

_____

WEEK 1 ~ MEMORY VERSE:

Matthew 22:37-39—The Great Commandment

"Jesus replied: 'Love the Lord your God with all your heart and with all your soul and with all your mind [and with all your strength].' This is the first and greatest commandment. And the second is like it"

"See You At The Pole" is a wonderful ministry that has greatly impacted the nation and the world. It is important that prayer continue all year long. Let's keep **"See You At The Pole"** alive all year.

S.Y.A.T.P. OR WE PRAY DAY

Meet every Wednesday, or another day that works for you – or every day – at the flagpole, or choose another place, that works for your situation. When you meet, pray for your campus. Many students have realized the benefits of meeting somewhere on campus every day. Be sure to invite other Christian clubs and students to join you.

In one city the students met every day in the lunchroom and fasted lunch together. They would share testimonies, pray, read God's word together. They saw so much happen in each of the schools that at the end of the 40-Days they didn't want to stop.

They organized themselves as "United Ignited" and continued to meet all year. Each week they would choose something new to fast, and devise their own assignments. They would also meet on Friday nights for worship and prayer. All of this was student initiated and student led.

Pray that God will start something through your group that will become a legacy.

    1. Discuss the weekly assignments.

    2. Share testimonies and pray for your campus.

    3. Pray for needs of your campus and of individual students.

    4. If the number of students is large, you can pray in groups of 3-5.

SOCIAL MEDIA ASSIGNMENT - Invite all of your twitter followers and facebook friends to join in the prayer

> **Hebrews 10:25** *"Let us not give up meeting together, as some are in the habit of doing, but let us encourage one another—and all the more as you see the Day approaching."*

HOMESCHOOLERS

If you're doing this with other homeschool students choose a place to meet, or if you can join friends at a local school, find out when and where they are meeting. You can also do this as a family. If you are part of a youth group maybe you can meet with a friend there and call that "The Point."

JOURNAL

Who came out to pray? Who can I invite to join me in the future?

_____

_____

_____

_____

_____

QUOTE

"Oh how few find time for prayer! There is time for everything else, time to sleep and time to eat, time to read the newspaper and the novel, time to visit friends, time for everything else under the sun, but no time for prayer, the most important of all things, the one great essential!" —OSWALD SMITH

PRAYER

_____

_____

_____

_____

_____

_____

WEEK 1 ~ MEMORY VERSE:

Matthew 22:37-39—The Great Commandment

"Jesus replied: 'Love the Lord your God with all your heart and with all your soul and with all your mind [and with all your strength].' This is the first and greatest commandment. And the second is like it"

Your **principal** and other **administrators** have a very difficult job. They play a very important role on your campus. When students bless, pray for, and serve their administrators, it has an amazing impact on their school.

PRINCIPAL/ADMINISTRATOR DAY

The following are some ways to pray for, to bless, and to serve your principal.

1. Pray for your principal, vice principal, and other support staff.

2. Write a note to let them know you are praying for them.

3. Visit them in their offices and ask how you can pray for them.

4. Bring them a gift or serve them.

5. If you have been at odds with someone in leadership, make things right. Apologize to that person. *Remember to make people's jobs easier, not harder.

SOCIAL MEDIA ASSIGNMENT - Post something encouraging about your principle

Romans 13:1-3 *"Everyone must submit himself to the governing authorities, for there is no authority except that which God has established. The authorities that exist have been established by God. Consequently, he who rebels against the authority is rebelling against what God has instituted, and those who do so will bring judgment on themselves. For rulers hold no terror for those who do right, but for those who do wrong. Do you want to be free from fear of the one in authority? Then do what is right and he will commend you."*

Pray these passages over your leaders.

Ephesians 1:17-20 *Ephesians 3:16-20*

Philippians 1:8-11 *Colossians 1:9-11*

I Thessalonians 3:12-13 *2 Thessalonians 1:1-11*

HOMESCHOOLERS

Who are the people who are in charge in your life? Your parents? A tutor or pastor? Maybe the leader at the co-op class you go to. Take the time to bless them today, as well.

JOURNAL

My Administrators' needs:

_____

_____

_____

_____

_____

QUOTE

"When a believing person prays, great things happen."
—JAMES THE LESS / MARTYRED FOR CHRIST / 63A.D.

PRAYER

_____

_____

_____

_____

_____

_____

WEEK 1 ~ MEMORY VERSE:

Matthew 22:37-39—The Great Commandment

"Jesus replied: 'Love the Lord your God with all your heart and with all your soul and with all your mind [and with all your strength].' This is the first and greatest commandment. And the second is like it"

Unforgiveness is like pouring a glass of poison to hurt the other person and drinking it yourself. It only hurts you.

FORGIVENESS DAY!
(Seeking forgiveness and giving forgiveness)

Jesus encouraged us in the Sermon on the Mount that it is critical to make things right with people whom we have offended. It is more important than making sacrifices, such as fasting. Ask God if there is anyone (student, teacher, parent, etc.) from whom you need to ask forgiveness. Then, "just do it." One girl made up with a friend she hadn't spoken to in over a year. They are now best friends.

A great way to begin the conversation is to say, "I realize that I have hurt you or disappointed you with my actions. Will you forgive me?"

You may need to forgive someone else. Forgiving those who have hurt us could be difficult. No doubt, many of you have been wronged by a parent, friend, other relative, or some other individual. Some of you have experienced abuse. God will help you. When you forgive, it helps you heal. Forgiveness is crucial. For more on forgiveness see Appendix 1 on page 114.

1. Make a list of people you haven't forgiven.

   (Use a separate piece of paper or the space in your journal.)

2. Ask God to help you forgive them.

3. Then, with your will, pray, "I forgive _____ " (Insert his or her name) completely and I let go of all bitterness.

4. Scratch each individual's name off your list after you have forgiven him or her. If you write it on a piece of paper feel free to burn it.

5. If it seems necessary, tell each person that you forgive him or her.

SOCIAL MEDIA ASSIGNMENT - Post this verse

Matthew 5:23-24 *"Therefore, if you are offering your gift at the altar and there remember that your brother has something against you, leave your gift there in front of the altar. First go and be reconciled to your brother; then come and offer your gift."*

Matthew 6:12 *"Forgive us our debts, as we also have forgiven our debtors."*

JOURNAL

_____
_____
_____
_____
_____
_____
_____

QUOTE

"To be a Christian means to forgive the inexcusable, because God has forgiven the inexcusable in you."

—C.S. Lewis

PRAYER

_____
_____
_____
_____
_____
_____
_____

WEEK 1 ~ MEMORY VERSE:

Matthew 22:37-39—The Great Commandment

"Jesus replied: 'Love the Lord your God with all your heart and with all your soul and with all your mind [and with all your strength].' This is the first and greatest commandment. And the second is like it"

[ASSIGNMENT] WEEK 1 ~ DAY 7 ~ SATURDAY ____/____/____

DEMOLITION DAY

Look at your bedroom, car, and living room. Ask Jesus if anything is there which displeases Him. Ask Him to reveal what He wants you to get rid of. Then get rid of it! If you find this process hard, then ask God to help you love Him more than these things that displease Him.

Some students have been led to get rid of

__ CDs
__ Cigarettes
__ Ouija boards/occult

__ Video Games
__ Drugs
__ Videos

__ Magazines
__ Books
__ Cable

__ Revealing clothing
__ Social Media
__ Food

__ Sexual Temptations
__ Sports
__ Other_____

Check off things that apply. Don't sell them! Be creative and demolish them. Make it fun, do it with a friend. DVDs, magazines and books make good bonfires (get Mom's permission)

SOCIAL MEDIA ASSIGNMENT - Post a video of you destroying stuff on Vine/Instagram/ Facebook

> ***Acts 19:19*** *"Also, many of those who had practiced magic brought their books together and burned them in the sight of all. And they counted up the value of them, and it totaled fifty thousand pieces of silver."*

> ***Matthew 5:29*** *"If your right eye causes you to stumble, gouge it out and throw it away. It is better for you to lose one part of your body than for your whole body to be thrown into hell." (Be sure to get your mom's permission before gouging out your eye!)*

> ***Psalm 119:9-11*** *"How can a young man keep his way pure? By living according to your word. I seek you with all my heart; do not let me stray from your commands. I have hidden your word in my heart that I might not sin against you."*

What needs to be eliminated from my room, home, car or life?

_____

_____

_____

_____

_____

_____

_____

_____

QUOTE

"Fight and you may die, run and you'll live. . . A little while. . . but lying on your death bed many years from now, would you be willing to trade all of the days from this day to that, for one chance, just one chance to come back here and tell our enemies that they may take our lives but they'll never take our freedom."

—WILLIAM WALLACE, MAIN CHARACTER FROM THE MOVIE, "BRAVEHEART."

PRAYER

_____

_____

_____

_____

_____

_____

WEEK 1 ~ MEMORY VERSE:

Matthew 22:37-39—The Great Commandment

"Jesus replied: 'Love the Lord your God with all your heart and with all your soul and with all your mind [and with all your strength].' This is the first and greatest commandment. And the second is like it"

Did you know that **93%** of boys, and **62%** of girls are exposed to internet porn before the age of 18? If that wasn't bad enough, **50%** of all Christian men and **20%** of all Christian women are currently addicted to pornography! God loves you and will forgive your sin but the affects can be devastating in your life and in future relationships – but God can set you free.

JOB 31 DAY

We have all heard the stats about pre-marital sex, but what we don't realize is how far we have fallen in other areas. So, today you're going to change that! You're going to take steps to get free from any addictions to pornography; make a covenant to say no to pre-marital sex in any form. If you have already fallen short ask for forgiveness, receive His forgiveness, forgive yourself and the other person.

Finally, you are going to fight lust with everything you have. Matthew 5:29 says that *"If your right eye causes you to sin you should gouge is out. For it is better for you to lose one part of your body than your whole body to be thrown into hell."* Basically this scripture says you do whatever it takes to beat this sin!

1. If you struggle with pornography get help! Get computer programs like Covenant Eyes, or xxxchurch.com. Delete any apps that you may have used before. If you have to, fast the Internet for a short time.

2. In Job 31:1, Job made a covenant with his eyes not to look at a women lustfully. Do the same, and pray for Gods help and protection over your eyes. Say, "I covenant with my eyes, before God, that I will not let any unwholesome thing into my eyes."

3. If you've had pre-marital sex, ask God's forgiveness, receive His forgiveness, forgive the person you had sex with, break any ungodly soulties. And if you're currently in a physical relationship, seek help from your spiritual leader on how to resolve the problem.

4. Pray against this scheme of the enemy at work in your school.

DECLARE THESE PASSAGES:

Job 31:1 - NIV *"I made a covenant with my eyes, not to look lustfully at a young woman."*

Matthew 5:28 *"anyone who looks at a women lustfully has already committed adultery with her in his heart."*

JOURNAL

What are some things you can do to get freedom in this area?

_____

_____

_____

_____

_____

_____

_____

_____

QUOTE

"Love is patient . . . love is kind."
—the BIBLE.

PRAYER

_____

_____

_____

_____

_____

_____

WEEK 2 ~ MEMORY VERSE:

Matthew 28:19-20—The Great Commission

"Therefore go and make disciples of all nations, baptizing them in the name of the Father and of the Son and of the Holy Spirit, and teaching them to obey everything I have commanded you. And surely I [Jesus] am with you always, to the very end of the age."

[ASSIGNMENT]

JERICHO MARCH DAY

Read Joshua chapters 1 and 6. God promised Joshua that if he was bold and courageous to go into the land, God was going to give him every place his foot touched. In the same way, if you will join with a friend or a group of Christians and walk around your campus, praying for it, you will see God begin to change your school.

1. Pray for your fellow students, teachers, and administrators.

2. Ask God to turn the lost on your campus to Christ.

3. Ask God to set free students who are enslaved to addictions.

4. Ask God to set the Christians at your school on fire.

5. Ask each person you see if you can pray for any needs in his or her life.

DECLARE THESE PASSAGES:

Joshua 6:2-5 "See, I have delivered Jericho into your hands, along with its king and its fighting men. March around the city once with all the fighting men. Do this for six days. Have seven priests carry trumpets of rams' horns in front of the ark. On the seventh day, march around the city seven times, with the priests blowing the trumpets. When you hear them sound a long blast on the trumpets, have all the people give a loud shout; then the wall of the city will collapse and the people will go up, every man straight in."

I John 1:7 "But if we walk in the light, as he is in the light, we have fellowship with one another, and the blood of Jesus, his Son, purifies us from all sin."

Luke 2:52 "And Jesus grew in wisdom and stature, and in favor with God and men."

2 Timothy 1:7, KJV "For God hath not given us the spirit of fear; but of power, and of love, and of a sound mind."

HOMESCHOOLERS

This is another easy thing for you to do! You can walk around your block, or even the whole neighborhood if you want. OR, if you want, get together with some other Homeschoolers and walk around your CHURCH! Pray and believe that God WILL do things as you pray.

JOURNAL

What or who did God lay on your heart to pray for?

_____

_____

_____

_____

_____

QUOTE

"The church that is arising is stronger, healthier, mightier and capable of transforming our cities by changing the spiritual climate."

—ED SILVOSO, AUTHOR OF THAT NONE SHOULD PERISH & PRAYER EVANGELISM

PRAYER

_____

_____

_____

_____

_____

_____

WEEK 2 ~ MEMORY VERSE:

Matthew 28:19-20—The Great Commission

"Therefore go and make disciples of all nations, baptizing them in the name of the Father and of the Son and of the Holy Spirit, and teaching them to obey everything I have commanded you. And surely I [Jesus] am with you always, to the very end of the age."

As Christians we are called to follow Jesus and to be like Jesus. Nothing epitomizes the life of Jesus more than unconditional love for everyone. By definition God is love. His love is not conditional upon how you act or what you do. Whether you're the perfect little church girl or the rebel, he loves you!

WOMAN AT THE WELL DAY

As Christians we need to learn how to love everyone, not just people that we like. Learn love for the outcasts – the people no one talks to, the ones who are uncool, not popular or good-looking even the one who annoys you a little.

Read John Chapter 4. Christians have earned a bad reputation when it comes to loving others who don't believe the way we do. Everyone has sinned and fallen short of the glory of God. Too often Christians come across judgmental, whether that is their intention or not. Jesus spent his time around sinners, not to condemn them but to show love and witness to them.

Ask for forgiveness for anytime you have not shown love to anyone!

1. Pray for opportunities to show love to those who need it, people who are bullied, or anyone else who needs a friend.

2. Also pay attention to anything you say "jokingly" to your friends or anyone, that could be mean or offensive

3. Forgive anyone who bullied you or who did not show love in the past.

SOCIAL MEDIA ASSIGNMENT - Be an encouragement to people today on social media. Look for opportunities to compliment people and just be a light.

> *John 8:10-11 When Jesus had raised Himself up and saw no one but the woman, He said to her, "Woman, where are those accusers of yours? Has no one condemned you?" 11 She said, "No one, Lord." And Jesus said to her, "Neither do I condemn you; go and sin no more."*

A STRATEGY TO IMPACT YOUR WORLD FOR CHRIST

HOMESCHOOLERS

This will be an easy day for you to do. No matter where you go to school you will have an opportunity to show unconditional love to everyone, maybe it's your family or someone from church.

JOURNAL

Make a list of the people you haven't shown love to. How can you treat them differently?

_____

_____

_____

_____

_____

QUOTE

"God is Love."

—the BIBLE

PRAYER

_____

_____

_____

_____

_____

_____

_____

IMPORTANT NOTE: The next day needs some planning and preparation!

WEEK 2 ~ MEMORY VERSE:

Matthew 28:19-20—The Great Commission

"Therefore go and make disciples of all nations, baptizing them in the name of the Father and of the Son and of the Holy Spirit, and teaching them to obey everything I have commanded you. And surely I [Jesus] am with you always, to the very end of the age."

Today you're going to make the choice to not be a statistic. If you're in school, I'm sure you have heard statistics about drug use in schools and alcohol abuse. Today, you're going to have the choice to not be a statistic.

JUST SAY NO DAY

By the time high school students graduate, 72.5% of them will have consumed some alcohol, 46.3% will have smoked a cigarette and 36.8% will have tried marijuana.

1. Choose not to be a statistic. Choose to honor God by what you put into your body

2. Pray against substance abuse in your school.

3. Pray for anyone you know who is struggling in this area.

4. If you have struggled in this area seek help from a spiritual advisor.

5. This part of today's assignment is going to be a little different than the rest. It will take some guts to do this! You're going to need a white t-shirt, colorful sharpies, and some creativity.

Make a t-shirt which shows that you choose Jesus over anything else, and that you're brave enough to say no to drugs and alcohol. Let love triumph over condemnation.

SOCIAL MEDIA ASSIGNMENT - Post this verse.

> *1 Corinthians 6:19-20 "Do you not know that your bodies are temples of the Holy Spirit, who is in you, whom you have received from God? You are not your own; 20 you were bought at a price. Therefore honor God with your bodies."*

HOMESCHOOLERS

Your neighborhood is a great place to apply this day. Take time today to prayer walk your neighborhood, praying against substance abuse and anything else God lays on your heart.

JOURNAL

What are you going to put on your t-shirt? How can you make it creative?

_____

_____

_____

_____

_____

_____

_____

PRAYER

_____

_____

_____

_____

_____

_____

_____

_____

WEEK 2 ~ MEMORY VERSE:

Matthew 28:19-20—The Great Commission

"Therefore go and make disciples of all nations, baptizing them in the name of the Father and of the Son and of the Holy Spirit, and teaching them to obey everything I have commanded you. And surely I [Jesus] am with you always, to the very end of the age."

Teachers play a significant role in your life. If you will let God use you in their lives, you will see Him do miracles. Pray for them; they need it. Serve them, even if you find them tough to love. Bless them! In doing so, you will see them in a whole new way - and as an added benefit, they'll see you from a new perspective.

TEACHER DAY

You can do one or more of the following:

1. Pray for your teacher. Ask your teacher (s) how you can pray for them. Be sure to write down their request and pray for them.

2. It is good to give your teacher a simple note. Some students have included a small gift, a candy bar or a drink with their note. This can have a powerful impact on their lives.

3. Remember, inquire later regarding the prayer request.

4. It is easy to do this for a teacher that you like. Try to take extra measures to pray for, bless and serve those teachers that you find harder to like!

5. Instead of complaining about bad teachers, start to pray for them. You will be amazed at how they change.

6. If you have ever talked bad about your teachers, repent of this and ask God to forgive you. If necessary go to them and ask forgiveness.

SOCIAL MEDIA ASSIGNMENT - Post an encouragement to your teachers, maybe a thank you to a special teacher on your facebook or vine.

> **Galatians 6:6** *"Anyone who receives instruction in the word must share all good things with his instructor."*

HOMESCHOOLERS

You may not think about them in this way, but your mom and dad are your teachers! It can be an even harder job for them, especially if your family has kids in different grades. They really need for you to stop and thank them today for all they do. Pick a couple of things on the list to do for them today. Make it extra special.

JOURNAL

What can you do to improve or repair your relationships with teachers?

_____

_____

_____

_____

_____

QUOTE

"When a nation calls its prime men to battle, homes are broken, weeping sweethearts say their goodbyes, businesses are closed, college careers are wrecked, factories are refitted for wartime production, rationing and discomforts are accepted—all for war. Can we do less for the greatest fight that this world has ever known outside of the cross—this endtime siege on sanity, morality and spirituality?"

—LEONARD RAVENHILL, REVIVAL PREACHER 1900S

PRAYER

_____

_____

_____

_____

_____

_____

WEEK 2 ~ MEMORY VERSE:

Matthew 28:19-20—The Great Commission

"Therefore go and make disciples of all nations, baptizing them in the name of the Father and of the Son and of the Holy Spirit, and teaching them to obey everything I have commanded you. And surely I [Jesus] am with you always, to the very end of the age."

Meals are an important part of each day. When we think about eating a meal with someone, we usually choose to eat with our friends.

SHARE A MEAL FOR JESUS DAY

Today you are to take an opportunity to share a meal with someone who might not know the Lord.

1. Pray about who you will ask to either breakfast, lunch and or dinner. If today doesn't work for that person then you can set up a day that does work.

2. Don't feel pressure to start sharing the gospel with the person. If that happens then be ready. Instead, just seek to get to know the person.

3. If the person asks why you are doing this, tell them that you just want to show them that God loves them, no strings attached.

4. If you are comfortable with it, then you are encouraged to invite a homeless person to a meal. Taking them a meal and a gospel tract is great, but imagine if every homeless person on the streets of your city today had someone spend time with them, pray for them and give them a meal.

5. Send some money to a famine relief program somewhere, or to a homeless ministry in your city.

One student brought $20 to school, picked people at random, and bought their lunches. He had a blast and some great conversations about the Lord.

HOMESCHOOLERS

Ask your Mom and Dad if you can make a meal, or if you can go to a local fast-food restaurant and buy someone else's meal for them. When they ask why, tell them you wanted to show them God's love for them in a simple way!

JOURNAL

Who are you going to buy a Meal for today?

_____
_____
_____
_____
_____
_____
_____

QUOTE

"The church gives more time, thought and money to recreation and sports than to prayer."
—SAMUEL CHADWICK

PRAYER

_____
_____
_____
_____
_____
_____

WEEK 2 ~ MEMORY VERSE:

Matthew 28:19-20—The Great Commission

"Therefore go and make disciples of all nations, baptizing them in the name of the Father and of the Son and of the Holy Spirit, and teaching them to obey everything I have commanded you. And surely I [Jesus] am with you always, to the very end of the age."

[ASSIGNMENT]

What is the one thing you could do for your **parents** or **guardians** that would really bless and surprise them, and would demonstrate your love for them?

SERVE YOUR FAMILY DAY

Take the initiative to do something special without having to be asked. If you have done something that has caused strife in your home, confess it and ask forgiveness. If you are harboring unforgiveness, then forgive the parent or brother or sister toward whom you are bitter.

Here are some other suggestions: (Choose more than one.)

1. Babysit	6. Paint	11. Rake
2. Do laundry	7. Wash windows	12. Weed
3. Cook	8. Repair something	13. Wash cars
4. Mow yard	9. Wash dishes	14. Clean bathroom
5. Clean pool	10. Mop	15. Make something

Ask everyone in your family if there is anything you can work on to be a better sibling/son/daughter. Also, ask if there is anything you have done that hurt them. If they ask why, just say you want to be as much like Christ to them as possible.

SOCIAL MEDIA ASSIGNMENT - Tell the world about how much you love your family and what they mean to you.

> **Ephesians 6:2-3** *"Honor your father and mother'—which is the first commandment with a promise—that it may go well with you and that you may enjoy long life on the earth."*

HOMESCHOOLERS

Two girls from one youth group were serving their family during the 40-Days. Their unsaved father ended up coming to church and giving his life to Christ because of what he saw in his daughter's life. He told the youth pastor that watching his daughters made him realize that God was real.

JOURNAL

What's something special you can do for each member of your family?

_____

_____

_____

_____

_____

_____

_____

QUOTE

"Revival is living the Christ life in the home."

—JAMES A. STEWART

PRAYER

_____

_____

_____

_____

_____

_____

WEEK 2 ~ MEMORY VERSE:

Matthew 28:19-20—The Great Commission

"Therefore go and make disciples of all nations, baptizing them in the name of the Father and of the Son and of the Holy Spirit, and teaching them to obey everything I have commanded you. And surely I [Jesus] am with you always, to the very end of the age."

[ASSIGNMENT]

In today's fast-paced world we often find little time to talk to the people who live right next door to us. God wants to use you to minister to people in your neighborhood. You are the light. Don't let the light be hidden.

LIGHTHOUSE DAY II - "WE PRAY"

1. Take a walk around your neighborhood and pray for your neighbors. Pray especially for students who live in your neighborhood.

2. Ask God to bless them, even if you don't get along with them.

3. Ask God to give you chances to show them God's love in practical ways and to tell them about His love.

4. Look for opportunities to actually serve someone.

__ bake a pie	__ give a gift	__ tutor
__ mow a lawn	__ bring food	__ send a pizza
__ write a note	__ fix something	__ clean for them

SOCIAL MEDIA ASSIGNMENT - Take today to post any testimonies about what has taken place the last few days on social media.

One of the times that I did the 40-Day Revolution, on this day we ordered pizza – but we ordered an extra pizza to give to our neighbors, but we didn't know who we were going to give it to.

We just started walking around. No one answered at the first 2 doors we knocked on, but the third one we knocked opened, and in their hand they were holding their phone and a pizza hut pizza coupon.

They were about to order the exact same thing that we gave them! It was a great opportunity to meet a new family in the neighborhood and share with them about the 40 days and Jesus!

I'm not saying this will happen every time, but listen to God's voice and trust him.

JOURNAL

How many neighbors did you know before today? How can you change that?

_____
_____
_____
_____
_____
_____
_____
_____

QUOTE

"Love your neighbor as yourself."

—MATTHEW 22:39

PRAYER

_____
_____
_____
_____
_____
_____
_____
_____
_____

WEEK 3 ~ MEMORY VERSE:

Proverbs 18:21, KJV—Blessing Evangelism

"Death and Life are in the power of the tongue; and they that love it shall eat the fruit thereof."

[ASSIGNMENT]

Whenever an army strategically plans to take over a city, it locates the gates or the entry points into the city. **Controlling** what goes in and out provides a powerful advantage.

STORM THE GATES

It is time for us to seize that powerful advantage over our campuses, neighborhoods and cities, by praying in front of the gates or entry points into the schools, homes, and neighborhoods.

1. Pray in front of your school's main doorway and before the doors of your home.
2. Ask God to come and rule, to bring His protection, and to set angels as guards on your campus and home.
3. Some have chosen to anoint the door with oil to symbolize a dedication of the campus to God.
4. Ask for God's mercy on those who have sinned. Pray that any curses on your campus and home would be broken.
5. Ask God to guard the school and your home from evil and to prevent lies from being able to take root in people's lives.

SOCIAL MEDIA ASSIGNMENT -Your social media accounts are the gates to your beliefs, Take today to clean up all your accounts to glorify the lord. Delete pictures that don't glorify God. Delete likes or posts that God leads you to. Maybe even delete friends who don't honor God.

> *Genesis 24:60 ". . . may your offspring possess the gates of their enemies."*
>
> *Isaiah 26:2 "Open the gates that the righteous nation may enter, the nation that keeps faith."*
>
> *Matthew 16:16-18 ". . . You are the Christ, the Son of the living God." ". . . And on this rock I will build my church and the gates of Hades will not overcome it."*

HOMESCHOOLERS

Make sure you do this assignment! Pray over the entrance to your neighborhood and at the front door of your house. Ask God to protect your family as you do your schooling each day, and to let His peace fill your home.

JOURNAL

Who came to pray? What did you pray for?

_____

_____

_____

_____

_____

QUOTE

"When a nation calls its prime men to battle, homes are broken, weeping sweethearts say their goodbyes, businesses are closed, college careers are wrecked, factories are refitted for wartime production. Rationing and discomforts are accepted—all for war.

Can we do less for the greatest fight that this world has ever known outside of the cross—this end-time siege on sanity, morality and spirituality?"

—LEONARD RAVENHILL

PRAYER

_____

_____

_____

_____

_____

IMPORTANT NOTE: Tomorrow is cookie and doughnuts day. Plan ahead!

WEEK 3 ~ MEMORY VERSE:

Proverbs 18:21, KJV—Blessing Evangelism

"Death and Life are in the power of the tongue; and they that love it shall eat the fruit thereof."

Today's assignment will cost you some money and time, but it will be a blast. **Serving OTHERS** always costs us. This assignment is really fun when done as a youth group or club activity.

COOKIES/DOUGHNUTS DAY

It is great when youth pastors are able to help organize this project with the students. Have youth leaders or adult volunteers present to help at each of the schools represented by your youth group. Be sure to get the administrator's permission.

1. Bake or buy cookies, doughnuts or other baked goods.
2. Get to school early and distribute the goodies.
3. Another option is to distribute them during lunch time.
4. Tell people, "This is just to show you God loves you in tangible ways."
5. Create a Facebook event, and invite everyone from your school. It's a good way to get the word out, and to get people talking.

SSOCIAL MEDIA ASSIGNMENT - Invite everyone to the location where you will be giving away the goodies.

> *Think Ahead—Be thinking about what to do Saturday for Bless Dad Day and for Sunday's Serve Somebody Day.*

> *Matthew 20:26-28 ". . . whoever wants to become great among you must be your servant, and whoever wants to be first must be your slave—just as the Son of Man did not come to be served, but to serve, and to give his life as a ransom for many."*

HOMESCHOOLERS

This is a real simple one for you. Pick a couple of neighbors that you could bless with a snack break today. Maybe watch for someone mowing the lawn, or better yet have a snack made and packaged for the mailman! Attach a little note to tell them this is your way of letting them know how much God loves them.

JOURNAL

What did you bake or buy for today?

_____

_____

_____

_____

_____

_____

QUOTE

"Keep us little and unknown, prized and loved by God alone."

—CHARLES WESLEY, GREAT EVANGELIST

PRAYER

_____

_____

_____

_____

_____

_____

WEEK 3 ~ MEMORY VERSE:

Proverbs 18:21, KJV—Blessing Evangelism

"Death and Life are in the power of the tongue; and they that love it shall eat the fruit thereof."

[ASSIGNMENT] WEEK 3 ~ DAY 18 ~ WEDNESDAY ___/___/___
<small>[TODAY'S DATE]</small>

Christ was our example of a **humble servant**. The Word of God tells us that God loves the humble and gives them grace.

HUMILITY DAY

Few things are more humbling than taking out the trash and cleaning toilets. Today your main objective is to serve someone in humility.

1. Pick up trash and trays in and around the cafeteria that may have been left by others.

2. Ask people if you can clean up their trash and their trays for them. Tell people who ask why you are doing this, "I want to show you God's love in a practical way."

3. Do this task with humility, without expecting anything in return.

4. Ask your teacher if you can take out the trash for him or her.

5. Take out the trash for your mom and dad. Offer to take the trash out for your neighbors if it is trash day.

6. Jesus – who was God in human form – washed his disciples feet.

SOCIAL MEDIA ASSIGNMENT - Post this verse

Matthew 20:26-28 ". . . whoever wants to become great among you must be your servant, and whoever wants to be first must be your slave—just as the Son of Man did not come to be served, but to serve, and to give his life as a ransom for many."

See if you can out do him, and you will be rewarded

Think Ahead—Be thinking about what to do Saturday for Bless Dad Day and for Sunday's Serve Somebody Day.

JOURNAL

What can you do to show humility? Who do you need to humble yourself to?

_____

_____

_____

_____

_____

_____

QUOTE

"He is no fool who gives what he cannot keep to gain what He cannot lose."

—JIM ELLIOT, MISSIONARY MARTYRED BY THE AUCA INDIANS

PRAYER

_____

_____

_____

_____

_____

_____

WEEK 3 ~ MEMORY VERSE:

Proverbs 18:21, KJV—Blessing Evangelism

"Death and Life are in the power of the tongue; and they that love it shall eat the fruit thereof."

Today is dedicated to people who were once active in their faith **but are now M.I.A.,** those who used to walk with God and have now turned away.

M.I.A. (MISSING IN ACTION) DAY

Remember that anything God leads you to do must be done with humility, love, and a desire to restore individuals to faith. Many people have been spiritually wounded. Do not condemn or be judgmental.

1. Pray for people you know who are M.I.A.

2. Speak an encouraging word to them.

3. Listen to his or her story about how they were wounded.

4. Write a note to encourage them.

5. Try to build a relationship with them, so you can have a platform to invite them back.

SOCIAL MEDIA ASSIGNMENT -Invite your twitter Followers and Facebook Friends to join you at church this coming week! If they can't come, at least give them the link to the service.

Gods grace is enough, look at how He forgave Israel and kept pursuing them, in the same way God never stops pursuing you.

> **Galatians 6:1-2** *"Brothers, if someone is caught in a sin, you who are spiritual should restore him gently. But watch yourself, or you also may be tempted. Carry each other's burdens, and in this way you will fulfill the law of Christ."*

Who are the M.I.A.s and how will you bless them?

_____

_____

_____

_____

_____

_____

QUOTE

"The whole history of the Church is one long story of this tendency to settle down on this earth and to become conformed to this world, to find acceptance and popularity here and to eliminate the element of conflict and of pilgrimage. That is the trend and the tendency of everything. Therefore outwardly, as well as inwardly, pioneering is a costly thing."

—T. AUSTIN SPARK

PRAYER

_____

_____

_____

_____

_____

_____

WEEK 3 ~ MEMORY VERSE:

Proverbs 18:21, KJV—Blessing Evangelism

"Death and Life are in the power of the tongue; and they that love it shall eat the fruit thereof."

Food is a blessing that many Americans take for granted, when in reality most of the world and a large percentage of Americans aren't sure where there next meal is coming from.

I WAS HUNGRY DAY

You are halfway to finishing the 40 days! Yeah!!! Keep it up!

For the next seven school days, you will be ministering to Jesus in practical ways. Read **Matthew 25:31-46**. Remember that when you serve others, you are serving Jesus. Each day you will be ministering to a different need. Realize as you serve others who you are really serving. Consider the following options:

1. Fast from food for the day, and use the money you save to buy someone a lunch.
    a. If the person asks why, reply "Just because I want you to know that God loves you in a practical way. No strings attached."
    b. If the person wants you to sit with him or her, then do so and pray for a chance to share more about God's love with him or her.
2. If you know where a homeless person is, buy a meal and bring it to him or her.
3. Make a meal for a needy family or buy them some groceries.
4. Send some money to a famine relief program.

SOCIAL MEDIA ASSIGNMENT

Post this verse:

Matthew 25:35,40 *"For I was hungry and you gave me something to eat . . . whatever you did for one of the least of these brothers of mine, you did for me."*

HOMESCHOOLERS

Ask your Mom and Dad if you can go to a local fastfood restaurant and buy someone else's meal for them. When they ask why, tell them you're showing God's love for them in a simple way!

JOURNAL

Do you take food for granted?

_____

_____

_____

_____

_____

_____

QUOTE

"By the time the average Christian gets his temperature up to normal, everybody thinks he has a FEVER!"

—WATCHMAN NEE, CHINESE AUTHOR AND LEADER

PRAYER

_____

_____

_____

_____

_____

_____

WEEK 3 ~ MEMORY VERSE:

Proverbs 18:21, KJV—Blessing Evangelism

"Death and Life are in the power of the tongue; and they that love it shall eat the fruit thereof."

[ASSIGNMENT]

Do something to get closer to your dad. If you don't know your earthly father, or if he has passed away, choose a father figure, or your **Heavenly Father.**

LOVE DAD DAY

If Dad is out of town, choose another day, or do something that he will appreciate upon his return. If there is strife between you that you need to clear up, do what you can.

If you have wronged your father, then ask his forgiveness. If he has hurt or wronged you, then forgive him, and let him know it.

1. Tell him how special he is
2. Show love with actions
3. Write an encouraging note
4. Serve him in a practical way
5. Mow the lawn
6. Wash the car
7. Take him out for breakfast

8. Treat him to lunch
9. Take him out for dinner
10. Babysit siblings
11. Change the oil
12. Buy a gift
13. Take him fishing
14. Other _____ _____

SOCIAL MEDIA ASSIGNMENT - Post something on your dad's wall about how much you love him.

> *Deuteronomy 4:16 'Honor your father and your mother, as the LORD your God commanded you, that your days may be long, and that it may go well with you in the land that the LORD your God is giving you."*

> *Malachi 4:5-6 "See, I will send you the prophet Elijah before that great and dreadful day of the Lord comes. He will turn the hearts of the fathers to their children, and the hearts of the children to their fathers; or else I will come and strike the land with a curse."*

JOURNAL

How will you bless my dad or guardian the most today?

_____
_____
_____
_____
_____
_____

QUOTE

"A baptism of holiness, a demonstration of godly living is the crying need of our day."
—DUNCAN CAMPBELL, MISSIONARY AND AUTHOR

PRAYER

_____
_____
_____
_____
_____
_____

WEEK 3 ~ MEMORY VERSE:

Proverbs 18:21, KJV—Blessing Evangelism

"Death and Life are in the power of the tongue; and they that love it shall eat the fruit thereof."

[ASSIGNMENT]

Ask God to show you a way to serve someone who is in need today. Since it is also a **"Lighthouse Day"**, make sure at least part of the application is within your Lighthouse worksheet. Also seek to add two new names and their needs to your list.

LIGHTHOUSE DAY III - "SERVE SOMEBODY DAY"

1. Take food to a homeless
2. Visit a nursing home
3. Visit an elderly neighbor
4. Mow a neighbor's lawn
5. Clean a neighbor's pool
6. Bake cookies for someone
7. Baby-sit for free
8. Help a single mom with her kids

SOCIAL MEDIA ASSIGNMENT - Post any testimonies of what has taken place

James 1:27 *"Religion that God our Father accepts as pure and faultless is this; to look after orphans and widows in their distress and to keep oneself from being polluted by the world."*

Use some time today to:

1. Pray for the needs on your lighthouse sheet.
2. Write a note to one or more students.
3. Call the person God lays on your heart.

LIGHTHOUSE

1st Period

Your Desk

2nd Period

Your Desk

3rd Period

Your Desk

4th Period

Your Desk

5th Period

Your Desk

6th Period

Your Desk

JOURNAL

Who will you serve today, and how will you serve them?

_____

_____

_____

_____

_____

_____

QUOTE

"What you have done to the least of these you have done unto me."

—JESUS

PRAYER

_____

_____

_____

_____

_____

_____

IMPORTANT NOTE: Tomorrow is "I Was Thirsty Day." Plan ahead!

WEEK 4 ~ MEMORY VERSE:

John 13:14-15—Servant Evangelism

"Now that I, your Lord and Teacher, have washed your feet, you also should wash one another's feet. I have set you an example that you should do as I have done for you."

[ASSIGNMENT]

As mentioned on Day 20, this week you will be serving Jesus by serving others. It may cost you a little bit, but this week will be a blast, and **it will bear a lot of fruit**.

I WAS THIRSTY DAY

People feel more comfortable receiving drinks if the beverages are in closed containers. Today you will give a drink to those who are thirsty. Remember that the greatest thirst people have is for living water. By serving them you will make them even thirstier for the truth. The following are some ideas.

1. Buy drinks for others and give them away at school, in your neighborhood, or at a sporting event.

2. It would be great to fill up a cooler with drinks, lemonade, and water. Bring cups for the drinks.

3. Tell people that what Jesus has can really satisfy the thirst in their souls and spirit. Or tell them that you used to be thirsty, but not anymore, because Jesus satisfied your spiritual thirst.

4. Give a drink to your teacher, your mom, your dad, your boss, your friend, a stranger, and anyone God shows you who is thirsty.

5. Identify your local church, campus club, or youth group on a little address card as you hand out the drink.

SOCIAL MEDIA ASSIGNMENT - Post this scripture.

Matthew 25:35b & 40 "*. . . I was thirsty and you gave me something to drink . . . The king will reply, 'I tell you the truth, whatever you did for one of the least of these brothers of mine, you did for me.'*

See if you can coordinate with your youth pastor and other kids from your youth group. Make a sacrifice, don't do "just enough". Challenge your self and make a sacrifice; people will respond.

JOURNAL

Who can I get to do this with me?

_____

_____

_____

_____

_____

_____

QUOTE

"We have given too much attention to methods and to machinery and to resources, and too little to the Source of Power, the filling of the Holy Ghost."

—J. HUDSON TAYLOR, FOUNDER OF CHINA INLAND MISSION

PRAYER

_____

_____

_____

_____

_____

_____

WEEK 4 ~ MEMORY VERSE:

John 13:14-15—Servant Evangelism

"Now that I, your Lord and Teacher, have washed your feet, you also should wash one another's feet. I have set you an example that you should do as I have done for you."

In what ways could you bless, serve, pray for, or tell a stranger of God's love today?

I WAS A STRANGER DAY

Today you will serve Jesus by reaching out to a stranger. There are many ways that you could do this. Ask God to give you a creative way to invite a stranger into your life, circle of friends, club, or youth group.

1. Ask God to show you a stranger who needs someone to reach out to him or her and to reveal how you can bless him or her.

2. If needed, offer a ride to him or her (only if you are over sixteen with a valid driver's license and have a vehicle, of course!)

3. Invite your new friend to your table for lunch.

4. Invite them into your home or your circle of friends.

5. Meet a new neighbor, or someone who has been in the neighborhood for years, but you do not know them.

6. If you don't feel the Holy Spirit leading you towards someone, there is always that kid who sits by himself during lunch. Go talk to him and sit with him, or invite him to sit with you.

SOCIAL MEDIA ASSIGNMENT - Post this scripture.

> *Matthew 25:35a & 40* "*. . . I was a stranger and you invited me in . . . The King will reply, 'I tell you the truth, whatever you did for one of the least of these brothers of mine, you did for me.'*

See if you can coordinate with your youth pastor and other kids from your youth group. Make a sacrifice, don't do "just enough". Challenge your self and make a sacrifice; people will respond.

A STRATEGY TO IMPACT YOUR WORLD FOR CHRIST

HOMESCHOOLERS

Maybe there is someone at your church or in your neighborhood that you haven't met yet, or there may be someone who looks like they need a friend. We want you to do what you can to get to know someone new. Many Homeschoolers go to a coop, or get together in large groups for sports or other activities. If today is a day you do that, make sure you meet someone new.

JOURNAL

Who is a stranger to me at school, in my neighborhood, or at work?

_____

_____

_____

_____

_____

_____

QUOTE

"We socialists would have nothing to do if you Christians had continued the revolution begun by Jesus."

—SPOKEN IN THE 1920S BY A LEADING SOCIALIST

PRAYER

_____

_____

_____

_____

_____

_____

WEEK 4 ~ MEMORY VERSE:

John 13:14-15—Servant Evangelism

"Now that I, your Lord and Teacher, have washed your feet, you also should wash one another's feet. I have set you an example that you should do as I have done for you."

Believe that God not only ***can*** heal the sick, but that He ***will*** heal the sick.

I WAS SICK AND YOU VISITED DAY

Today you will have the chance again to serve Jesus in practical ways through caring for any who are sick. Read accounts of Jesus healing the sick to build your faith today.

1. Ask God to show you a stranger who needs someone to reach out to him or her and to reveal how you can bless him or her.

2. If needed, offer a ride to him or her (only if you are over sixteen with a valid driver's license and have a vehicle, of course!)

3. Invite your new friend to your table for lunch.

4. Invite them into your home or your circle of friends.

5. Meet a new neighbor, or someone who has been in the neighborhood for years, but you do not know them.

6. If you don't feel the Holy Spirit leading you towards someone, there is always that kid who sits by himself during lunch. Go talk to him and sit with him, or invite him to sit with you.

SOCIAL MEDIA ASSIGNMENT - Post this scripture.

> ***Matthew 25:36b, 40*** *"I was sick and you looked after me." ". . . I tell you the truth, whatever you did for one of the least of these brothers of mine, you did for me."*

> ***Think ahead:*** *Also be thinking of how you can bless Mom on Saturday and whom you will invite to church on Sunday.*

One Girl got to pray for her friend's niece who was scheduled to have surgery the next day. The following Monday, the girl told her friend that her niece had been healed, and didn't even have the surgery. They made so much noise the teacher asked if she wanted to share with the whole class what they were talking about. She said, "Sure!"

As a result of her faith and willingness to obey the Lord, she was able to share with her whole class about how God had healed her friend's niece.

JOURNAL

Who can you pray for? Do you have faith that God WILL heal them?

_____

_____

_____

_____

_____

_____

QUOTE

". . . in this night the dawn is about to break . . . God is recruiting an army of recklessly abandoned youth, completely devoted to Himself. They know what it is to love much because they have been forgiven much."

—LOU ENGLE, YOUTH EVANGELIST AND AUTHOR

PRAYER

_____

_____

_____

_____

_____

_____

WEEK 4 ~ MEMORY VERSE:

John 13:14-15—Servant Evangelism

"Now that I, your Lord and Teacher, have washed your feet, you also should wash one another's feet. I have set you an example that you should do as I have done for you."

[ASSIGNMENT]

Don't give things that are dirty, badly worn, or not any good. Give something worthy of Jesus.

YOU CLOTHED ME DAY

Today you will serve Jesus by giving away clothes to those in need. Remember that in serving others, you serve Jesus. Ask God, and He will show you what you should give.

1. Clean out your closet and give clothes away to the needy.

2. Buy something nice for someone who may not have much.

3. Start a clothing collection for a local charity at school, in your youth group, or in your neighborhood.

4. Find a homeless person. Find out that person's shoe size, shirt or pant size, and buy them something. Remember, some have given to angels without knowing it. Serve others as if they were Jesus.

SOCIAL MEDIA ASSIGNMENT - Post this scripture.

Matthew 25:36a, 40 "I needed clothes and you clothed me." . . . I tell you the truth, whatever you did for one of the least of these brothers of mine, you did for me." One Girl got to pray for her friend's niece who was scheduled to have surgery the next day. The following Monday, the girl told her friend that her niece had been healed, and didn't even have the surgery. They made so much noise the teacher asked if she wanted to share with the whole class what they were talking about. She said, "Sure!"

One day on the way home from a basketball practice my brother saw a homeless man shivering in the cold, so he took off his sweater and gave it to the man!

Do you have an excess of clothes? More shoes then you can wear in a month?

_____

_____

_____

_____

_____

_____

QUOTE

"We Christians have given Calvary to the Communists. They accept deprivation and death to spread their gospel, while we Christians reject any gospel that does not major on healing and happiness."

—GEORGE E. FAILLING

PRAYER

_____

_____

_____

_____

_____

_____

WEEK 4 ~ MEMORY VERSE:

John 13:14-15—Servant Evangelism

"Now that I, your Lord and Teacher, have washed your feet, you also should wash one another's feet. I have set you an example that you should do as I have done for you."

Sometimes you may feel like a **prisoner** at school. God may even give you a creative idea as to how you can minister to fellow students who are in detention at school.

I WAS IN PRISON AND YOU VISITED ME DAY

Today's assignment will be more difficult than most. Today you need to ask the Lord how to serve Jesus by serving those who are in prison. You may be considered too young to write to prisoners or to make jail/prison visits. You can still pray for prisoners. Check out one of these websites (http://www.prisonfellowship.org and http://kpmifoundation.org).

Some people are not in physical prisons but are bound in spiritual prisons. They may be addicted to drugs, alcohol, sex, or other sins that destroy them. Ministering opportunities include:

1. Give a Christian book or magazine to someone in detention.

2. Ask if you can take someone's place for detention. Jesus did this for you. We all deserved His punishment; He took it for us. (Be sure that your substitution is approved by authorities – or you may earn your own detention!

3. You may want to visit the websites:www.christianpenpals.com or www. prisonfellowship.org . They will help you to explore some ways to minister, and what to pray.

4. Ask whether your youth pastor has suggestions, or can set up an opportunity to visit a jail, or another way to minister to prisoners.

5. If none of the above work out for you, pray for those in prisons, and for those whose prisons are spiritual.

SOCIAL MEDIA ASSIGNMENT - Post this scripture.

> **Matthew 25:36c, 40** *"I was in prison and you came to visit me . . . I tell you the truth, whatever you did for one of the least of these brothers of mine, you did for me."*

JOURNAL

Do you know anyone who feels like they are stuck in prison?

_____

_____

_____

_____

_____

_____

QUOTE

"Remember the Lord's people who are in jail and be concerned for them. Don't forget those who are suffering, but imagine that you are there with them."

—PAUL THE APOSTLE (HEBREWS 13:2, CEV)

PRAYER

_____

_____

_____

_____

_____

_____

WEEK 4 ~ MEMORY VERSE:

John 13:14-15—Servant Evangelism

"Now that I, your Lord and Teacher, have washed your feet, you also should wash one another's feet. I have set you an example that you should do as I have done for you."

Love your mother. If she doesn't know Him, you could lead the way.

LOVE YOUR MOM DAY

Do something to make life easier for your Mom, Stepmom, or guardian. Do something to demonstrate your love for her. There are few people in this world, if any, who have done more for you than your mom. God's Word promises us a blessing if we honor our fathers and mothers. Here are a few suggestions:

1. Give her flowers
2. Do your chores
3. Take her shopping
4. Write her a note
5. Clean your room
6. Wash dishes
7. Do the laundry
8. Wash windows
9. Buy a gift
10. Let her take a nap
11. Babysit for her
12. Wash her car
13. Write a song
14. Write a poem
15. Cook dinner

SOCIAL MEDIA ASSIGNMENT - Post something on your mom's wall about how much you love her and what she means to you

Proverbs 10:1 *"A wise son brings joy to his father, but a foolish son grief to his mother."*

Proverbs 31:26-31 *"She speaks with wisdom, and faithful instruction is on her tongue. She watches over the affairs of her household and does not eat the bread of idleness. Her children arise and call her blessed; her husband also, and he praises her: Many woman do noble things, but you surpass them all." Charm is deceptive, and beauty is fleeting; but a woman who fears the Lord is to be praised. Give her the reward she has earned, and let her works bring her praise at the city gate. *

"My mother was the most beautiful woman I ever saw. All I am I owe to my mother. I attribute all my success in life to the moral, intellectual and physical education I received from her."

- George Washington

JOURNAL

What can I do that would show my mom or guardian I really love her?

_____

_____

_____

_____

_____

_____

QUOTE

"Many do not respond to the Gospel we preach because we do not love them as much as we love ourselves—and that contaminates our message."

—ED SILVOSO

PRAYER

_____

_____

_____

_____

_____

_____

IMPORTANT NOTE: Tomorrow is "Take A Friend to Curch Day." Plan ahead!

WEEK 4 ~ MEMORY VERSE:

John 13:14-15—Servant Evangelism

"Now that I, your Lord and Teacher, have washed your feet, you also should wash one another's feet. I have set you an example that you should do as I have done for you."

It's a great idea for your youth group to put forth a challenge with a special prize to be awarded to the individual or small group who brings the most visitors to church.

LIGHTHOUSE DAY IV - TAKE A FRIEND TO CHURCH DAY

Hopefully you have given consideration in advance regarding whom you will invite to church. If not, plan ahead for next week and invite someone to church next week.

This is a great chance to reach out to someone you have been praying for specifically. Now you can take the opportunity to invite that person to your church.

Ask your parents if they would be willing to drive any friends who need a ride before hand, so they don't have any excuses. The past 28 days have been leading up to this!

SOCIAL MEDIA ASSIGNMENT - Post something on your mom's wall about how much you love her and what she means to you

> **Hebrews 10:25** *"Let us not give up meeting together, as some are in the habit of doing, but let us encourage one another—and all the more as you see the Day approaching."*

LIGHTHOUSE

1st Period — Your Desk

2nd Period — Your Desk

3rd Period — Your Desk

4th Period — Your Desk

5th Period — Your Desk

6th Period — Your Desk

Who did you invite to church today? Who came?

_____

_____

_____

_____

_____

_____

QUOTE

"You can be sure that whoever brings the sinner back will save that person from death and bring about the forgiveness of many sins."

— JAMES 5:20, NLT

PRAYER

_____

_____

_____

_____

_____

_____

WEEK 5 ~ MEMORY VERSE:

II Corinthians 10:4,5, KJV—Prayer Evangelism

"For the weapons of our warfare are not carnal, but mighty through God to the pulling down of strong holds; casting down imaginations, and every high thing that exalteth itself against the knowledge of God, and bringing into captivity every thought to the obedience of Christ."

God invented time and all time is in his hands. We're supposed to give our lives to His service by furthering His kingdom. So, instead of finding excuses about why we didn't have time to spend with God, we're going to **MAKE time.**

BE WITH ME DAY

In todays culture there are millions of distractions and things that can get in the way of spending time with God. Whether its your phone, TV, video games, school or just the business of life it can be hard to make time for God. You know I hate that phrase "make time for God".

Today is about making time in your day to spend listening to God and reading His word. Everyone's schedules are different but you make time for things that are a priority.

1. Get up 15 min earlier so you can read your bible and start your day off right.

2. While riding or driving to school put an audio bible on. Lots of apps have this feature!

3. Bring your bible to school and during your lunch break read it! It could be a great conversation starter.

4. After school and homework don't go straight to your computer or TV. Put away the electronics and spend some quality time with God. Take time to read your bible, listen to what God has to say and right down what ever He speaks to you.

5. Pay attention to the things you would normally have done with your time, are they glorifying towards God?

SOCIAL MEDIA ASSIGNMENT - Fast (Don't go on) social media all day, instead spend the time with God. You will survive.

> **Philemon 1:6** *"I pray that you may be active in sharing your faith, so that you will have a full understanding of every good thing we have in Christ."*

JOURNAL

Do you Give God enough of your time?

_____

_____

_____

_____

_____

_____

QUOTE

"Every promise, every command in the Bible will be misunderstood unless we interpret it in the light of the Lord's command to Win the World for Him."

—ED SILVOSO

PRAYER

_____

_____

_____

_____

_____

_____

WEEK 5 ~ MEMORY VERSE:

II Corinthians 10:4,5, KJV—Prayer Evangelism

"For the weapons of our warfare are not carnal, but mighty through God to the pulling down of strong holds; casting down imaginations, and every high thing that exalteth itself against the knowledge of God, and bringing into captivity every thought to the obedience of Christ."

"Don't complain to yourselves that you can't go to the mission field! Thank God for bringing the **mission field** to you!"

- Brother Andrew, God's Smuggler

OPERATION WORLD DAY

God's concern is not only for your hometown, state, or country—He cares about the entire world, and has called us to have the same compassion. He has called us to go out into the entire world. Here are some practical ways to participate in Operation World Day!

1. Reach out to a foreign exchange student.

2. Pray for a missionary or a country. Think of practical needs.

3. Pray that more people would go abroad as missionaries—and ask God if He would have you to go.

4. Ask God if it is His will for you to go on a shortterm mission this summer.

5. "The justice Revolution" is another book that focuses entirely on injustice around the world, and on what you can do to pray and help out. If this is something that you are passionate about, you can order it on operationlightforce.com—and you may change not just your school, but the whole world.

SOCIAL MEDIA ASSIGNMENT - Post this verse

> **Matthew 28:19** *"Therefore, go and make disciples of all nations, baptizing them in the name of the Father and of the Son and of the Holy Spirit, and teaching them to obey everything I have commanded you. And surely I am with you always, to the very end of the age."*

> **Luke 10:2** - *Then He said to them, "The harvest truly is great, but the laborers are few; therefore pray the Lord of the harvest to send out laborers into His harvest.*

Who did you pray for today?

_____

_____

_____

_____

_____

_____

QUOTE

"The kingdom of God is a new order founded on the fatherly love of God, on redemption, justice and fellowship. It is meant to enter into all life, all nations, and all policies until the kingdom of this world becomes the kingdom of the Lord."

—ERIC LIDDELL, OLYMPIC GOLD-MEDAL WINNER AND MISSIONARY TO CHINA

PRAYER

_____

_____

_____

_____

_____

_____

WEEK 5 ~ MEMORY VERSE:

II Corinthians 10:4,5, KJV—Prayer Evangelism

"For the weapons of our warfare are not carnal, but mighty through God to the pulling down of strong holds; casting down imaginations, and every high thing that exalteth itself against the knowledge of God, and bringing into captivity every thought to the obedience of Christ."

No longer are Christians going to roll over and let Satan run their schools. No longer is he going to have his way in your school.

TAKE A STAND DAY

Today stand up for what you believe! Jesus took a stand in the temple. I'm not telling you to flip your desk, and yell, "Enough!" This is a follow up to Giants day. You have been praying about these giants in your school for 30 days, and today you take your stand.

In Luke 10:19, Jesus tells the 72 others that he has given them authority to trample snakes and scorpions, and to overcome all the power of the enemy—and that's exactly what you're going to do.

When you hear someone curse or use God's name in vain ask them nicely not to cuss. When you hear someone talking behind a teachers back, or slandering a classmate, tell him or her that gossiping is wrong and you don't think they should do it.

Stand against people lying, cheating, gossiping, fighting, showing bitterness, being lazy, or any evil that's going on at school. Pray against it. Tell your friends you don't like who they become when they drink or swear. Understand that you may face persecution for what you say and do, but the Bible says to count it as pure joy when you face persecution for Christ's name! Matthew 5:11-12

1. When your friends do something you know is not right, don't let it slide. Take a stand—but be careful to do it in LOVE!!!!

2. If anything came to mind that you knew was wrong but you didn't say anything, repent, and ask God what you should do.

3. Pray that your eyes will be open to the schemes of the enemy at work in your school, and ask God how you can stop them!

SOCIAL MEDIA ASSIGNMENT - Take a stand on your social media in a loving way .

A STRATEGY TO IMPACT YOUR WORLD FOR CHRIST

HOMESCHOOLERS

You can do this too, when your around your friends or maybe even with your family. Take a stand for what you believe in.

JOURNAL

What will you take a stand against?

_____

_____

_____

_____

_____

_____

_____

QUOTE

"Courage is what it takes to stand up and speak; courage is also what it takes to sit down and listen."

—WINSTON CHURCHILL

PRAYER

_____

_____

_____

_____

_____

_____

WEEK 5 ~ MEMORY VERSE:

II Corinthians 10:4,5, KJV—Prayer Evangelism

"For the weapons of our warfare are not carnal, but mighty through God to the pulling down of strong holds; casting down imaginations, and every high thing that exalteth itself against the knowledge of God, and bringing into captivity every thought to the obedience of Christ."

Racism is a curse on any land or people. America has come a long way, but there is still a long way to go toward destroying racism.

RECONCILIATION DAY

Today your goal is to move a step closer to destroying the barriers of racism by blessing, serving, and praying for someone of a race other than your own. Here are some suggestions:

1. Buy someone lunch
2. Pray for him or her
3. Seek to build a relationship
4. Listen to the person's concerns
5. Write an encouraging note
6. Give a gift
7. Pray with him or her

SOCIAL MEDIA ASSIGNMENT - Reach out to some people who you may have lost contact with or with whom there has been animosity.

Galatians 3:28 "There is neither Jew nor Greek, slave nor free, male nor female, for you are all one in Christ Jesus."

Ephesians 2:14-16 "For he himself is our peace, who has made the two one and has destroyed the barrier, the dividing wall of hostility, by abolishing in his flesh the law with its commandments and regulations. His purpose was to create in himself one new man out of the two, thus making peace, and in this one body to reconcile both of them to God through the cross, by which he put to death their hostility."

A STRATEGY TO IMPACT YOUR WORLD FOR CHRIST

JOURNAL

_____
_____
_____
_____
_____
_____

QUOTE

"The battle for the soul of this generation will not be won by a show of brute force. True conversion does not come by the sword but by the cross; not by taking of life but by the laying down of life."

—MICHAEL BROWN, AUTHOR AND SPEAKER

PRAYER

_____
_____
_____
_____
_____
_____

WEEK 5 ~ MEMORY VERSE:

II Corinthians 10:4,5, KJV—Prayer Evangelism

"For the weapons of our warfare are not carnal, but mighty through God to the pulling down of strong holds; casting down imaginations, and every high thing that exalteth itself against the knowledge of God, and bringing into captivity every thought to the obedience of Christ."

[ASSIGNMENT]

Too many Christians have spent their entire Christian lives living as slaves, even though Christ has already purchased their freedom. Christ came that you might have life, and have it more abundantly.

THE PURGE

Look at the list below and renounce all involvement in any area, according to God's leading. It is best to write out the specifics as He reveals them to you, renounce all, confess, and receive God's forgiveness—and then burn the list.

1. **Unforgiveness**: List all of the people from childhood to the present toward whom you have ever had any unforgiveness or resentment.

2. **The Occult:** Séances, Santeria, Dungeons and Dragons, Ouija boards, tarot cards, palm reading, psychics, witchcraft, and others.

3. **Sexual Sin:** premarital sex, lust, masturbation, adultery, pornography, homosexuality, lesbianism, rape, molestation.

4. **Soul Ties:** People that have had an ungodly control over you.

5. **Covenants, Vows, and Curses**: List all broken vows.

6. **Abuses:** verbal, emotional, sexual, psychological, or even spiritual hurts and rejections, both those received and those given.

7. **Death:** List deceased family members whose evil traits or character qualities have been attributed to you.

8. **Cursed objects and buildings:** List places of evil you have visited.

9. **Fears and Phobias:** List fears or phobias that are areas of struggle.

10. **Addictions:** List substances, foods, or behaviors that you find addictive.

SOCIAL MEDIA ASSIGNMENT - Purge yourself of any friends or people you follow on your social media accounts that are not glorifying to the Lord.

> **Daniel 4:27** "... Renounce your sins by doing what is right, and your wickedness by being kind to the oppressed. It may be that then your prosperity will continue."

JOURNAL

What do you need victory over?

_____

_____

_____

_____

_____

_____

QUOTE

"For everyone born of God overcomes the world. This is the victory that has overcome the world, even our faith."

—JOHN 5:4

PRAYER

_____

_____

_____

_____

_____

_____

WEEK 5 ~ MEMORY VERSE:

II Corinthians 10:4,5, KJV—Prayer Evangelism

"For the weapons of our warfare are not carnal, but mighty through God to the pulling down of strong holds; casting down imaginations, and every high thing that exalteth itself against the knowledge of God, and bringing into captivity every thought to the obedience of Christ."

[ASSIGNMENT]

HOME PRAYER WALK DAY

The place in which you spend most of your time (even if a lot of it is asleep) is in your home. Just as Joshua made the declaration, "As for me and my house we will serve the Lord," you must dedicate your home to the Lord. It is best if your parents can join you.

1. Pray in every room of your house or apartment. Pray that each room will be full of the peace and presence of the Lord.

2. If there is a room where many fights occur, when you pray in that room, ask God to forgive the angry words.

3. Pray that your home is hospitable and useful for leading people to Christ.

4. If your family and/or friends will join you, pray with your friends at each other's homes.

5. Walk the perimeter of your property praying over the land, and declaring that the land belongs to the Lord. Also repent of any sins that have happened on the land, and pray that God would restore the land

SOCIAL MEDIA ASSIGNMENT - Post this verse.

Romans 12:13. "Share with God's people who are in need. Practice hospitality."

A STRATEGY TO IMPACT YOUR WORLD FOR CHRIST

JOURNAL

Is there anything in your home that isn't glorifying to the lord?

_____

_____

_____

_____

_____

_____

QUOTE

"When the Spiritual climate changes for the better, so does everybody and everything in the city {home, dorm, apartment building}."

—ED SILVOSO, AUTHOR OF THAT NONE SHOULD PERISH & PRAYER EVANGELISM

PRAYER

_____

_____

_____

_____

_____

_____

WEEK 5 ~ MEMORY VERSE:

II Corinthians 10:4,5, KJV—Prayer Evangelism

"For the weapons of our warfare are not carnal, but mighty through God to the pulling down of strong holds; casting down imaginations, and every high thing that exalteth itself against the knowledge of God, and bringing into captivity every thought to the obedience of Christ."

[ASSIGNMENT]

LIGHTHOUSE DAY V - BLESS THE PASTOR DAY

Your pastor has a great responsibility for the souls of your church. God has surely used him in your life to speak to you. Even God's Word encourages us to honor those who have blessed us. Today make an extra special effort to bless your pastor and/or youth pastor.

1. Ask your pastor if there is anything you can do to serve him or her, or the church.

2. Write him or her an encouraging note.

3. Give him or her a gift.

4. Be an active member of the body of Christ.

5. Say something encouraging to him or her.

6. Give him or her a hug.

SOCIAL MEDIA ASSIGNMENT - Write something that will bless your pastor.

Also since today is a "Lighthouse Day," seek to meet or speak to two new neighbors whom you've not yet reached out to, and minister to their needs. Add their needs to your Lighthouse Prayer Guide.

> *I Corinthians 12:25-26* "So that there should be no division in the body, but that its parts should have equal concern for each other. If one part suffers, every part suffers with it; if one part is honored, every part rejoices with it."

JOURNAL

What did you do for your pastor?

_____
_____
_____
_____
_____
_____

QUOTE

"Come work for the Lord. The work is hard, the hours are long, and the pay is low, but the retirement benefits are out of this world."

—AUTHOR UNKNOWN

PRAYER

_____
_____
_____
_____
_____
_____

WEEK 6 ~ MEMORY VERSE:

II Timothy 1:13-14

"What you have heard from me, keep as the pattern of sound teaching, with faith and love in Christ Jesus. Guard the good deposit that was entrusted to you—guard it with the help of the Holy Spirit who lives in us."

School clubs are an important arena of interaction that can be used for God's purpose. Whether you are in a Christian club or any other type of club, you need to realize that you are to be a revolutionary for Jesus. Don't be molded into the norm. Set the standard!

CAMPUS CLUB DAY

Romans 12:2 (NIV) teaches us, "Do not conform to the pattern of this world, but be transformed by the renewing of your mind. Then you will be able to test and approve what God's will is—his good, pleasing and perfect will."

Today, find a way to bless your club, its leaders, and other members.

1. Pray for the leaders and sponsors of campus clubs. Pray for God's will to be done.

2. Attend the next meeting or start a campus club (i.e., Fellowship of Christian Athletes, Student Venture, Youth for Christ, or Young Life).

3. Some students have blessed clubs that Christians normally shun, like the gay club or some other club. Serving those whom others shun can open the door for powerful witnessing.

4. Start a Bible study with someone. Faith, commitment, and accountability found in meeting with others on campus are critical for your spiritual growth.

SOCIAL MEDIA ASSIGNMENT - Post this verse:

1 Peter 2:2 "Like newborn babies, crave pure spiritual milk, so that by it you may grow up in salvation."

Romans 12:11 "Never be lacking in zeal, but keep your spiritual fervor, serving the Lord."

HOMESCHOOLERS

This obviously would be a hard one for you to do – but it isn't impossible! Many of you are part of small group Bible studies in your church or youth group, or maybe you are part of a Scouting program, or take music or dance lessons after school. What about work – do you have a shift supervisor that you could bless today? Think really hard about who you can bless – and be creative!

JOURNAL

Are there any Christian clubs at your school?

_____

_____

_____

_____

_____

_____

QUOTE

"Jesus called his 12 disciples, knowing that the harvest was too plentiful for one person to reap it. He needed to work through others to minister to the masses."

—JOEL COMISKEY

PRAYER

_____

_____

_____

_____

_____

_____

WEEK 6 ~ MEMORY VERSE:

II Timothy 1:13-14

"What you have heard from me, keep as the pattern of sound teaching, with faith and love in Christ Jesus. Guard the good deposit that was entrusted to you— guard it with the help of the Holy Spirit who lives in us."

[ASSIGNMENT] WEEK 6 ~ DAY 38 ~ TUESDAY ___/___/___
[TODAY'S DATE]

You never know what a word of encouragement will mean to someone. People serve you every day without receiving even a word of appreciation. At least today, let's change our approach and become more grateful. Better yet, make it a habit.

CUSTODIAN/SUPPORT STAFF DAY

The custodians and support staff are the people who get very little recognition. The librarians, the food servers, or the janitor are too often not appreciated or acknowledged. Make their day by showing appreciation. You may decide to reach out to one person, or to several.

1. Ask if there is any way you can pray for them and then—if they will let you—pray.

2. Write a note to someone to let him or her know that he or she is special . . . and you prayed for him or her today.

3. Give a gift.

4. Buy lunch.

SOCIAL MEDIA ASSIGNMENT - Post this verse:

> *Ephesians 4:29* "Do not let any unwholesome talk come out of your mouths, but only what is helpful for building others up according to their needs, that it may benefit those who listen."

One young girl who brought a note of encouragement to one of the cleaning ladies saw her weeping as she read the note of gratitude for her work at the school. It was the beginning of a friendship that continued.

HOMESCHOOLERS

The world is FULL of people who do great things that people notice and praise them for. They could be firemen, the police, the military, nurses, doctors, politicians, or even movie actors. But what about the people who do things that we NEVER think about? The librarians, the garbage collectors, mail carriers, waitresses, and even people who work at the grocery store. They are all what we call "Unsung Heroes!" They are the people who don't get publicly recognized very often, but make a big difference. Make their day today by showing them your appreciation. You may decide to reach out to only one person or to several—you decide!

JOURNAL

What support staff can I bless/serve/pray for or communicate with today?

_____

_____

_____

_____

_____

_____

QUOTE

"This experience of ours is really worth taking a couple of bullets for. [If you do come,] don't think of returning, the revolution won't wait."

—CHE GUEVARA

INVITING HIS OLD FRIEND JULIO "EL GUACHO" CASTRO TO JOIN HIM IN CUBA

PRAYER

_____

_____

_____

_____

WEEK 6 ~ MEMORY VERSE:

II Timothy 1:13-14

"What you have heard from me, keep as the pattern of sound teaching, with faith and love in Christ Jesus. Guard the good deposit that was entrusted to you—guard it with the help of the Holy Spirit who lives in us."

One student brought his entire home computer to his youth pastor and told him to clean the hard drive off. He wanted to come clean, accept accountability for what he looked at online and commit for **40-Days** to be **free from all internet.** It radically changed this young man's life.

MEDIA FAST DAY

Today is the day to be free from every form of media, except for the Bible and your homework. For 24 hours abstain from:

___ TV and videos	___ Radio	___ Newspaper	
___ Audio CDs	___ Internet	___ Movies	___ Cell Phone
___ Facebook	___ Twitter	___ Snapchat	___ Instagram
___ Texting	___ IPods	___ Computer	

Devote the time you save to reading the Bible and praying. **(See Daniel 1:8-20.)**

Psalm 101:2-3 "I will be careful to lead a blameless life—when will you come to me? I will walk in my house with blameless heart. I will set before my eyes no vile thing."

SOCIAL MEDIA ASSIGNMENT - DO NOTHING!

What is the hardest media for me to fast, and why?

How did fasting media impact me?

How long can I go without any form of media? Why?

How much impact does media have on my life? For good? For bad?

JOURNAL

What did you do for your pastor?

_____

_____

_____

_____

_____

_____

QUOTE

"Prayer is the most unexplored area of the Christian life.
Prayer is the most powerful weapon of the Christian life.
Prayer is the most hell-feared battle in the Christian life.
Prayer is the most secret device of the Christian life.
Prayer is the most underestimated power in the Christian life.
Prayer is the most untaught truth in the Christian life.
Prayer is the most demanding exercise in the Christian life.
Prayer is the most neglected responsibility in the Christian life.
Prayer is the most conquering outreach in the Christian life.
Prayer is the most opposed warfare in the Christian life.
Prayer is the most far-reaching ministry in the Christian life."
—LEONARD RAVENHILL, AUTHOR AND EVANGELIST

PRAYER

_____

_____

_____

_____

_____

_____

WEEK 6 ~ MEMORY VERSE:

II Timothy 1:13-14

"What you have heard from me, keep as the pattern of sound teaching, with faith and love in Christ Jesus. Guard the good deposit that was entrusted to you—guard it with the help of the Holy Spirit who lives in us."

Jesus said," ***It is Finished***" while he was on the cross. But this was just the beginning of salvation.

IT IS FINISHED!

You may have finished the 40-Day Revolution, but it is really just the start. Think about what will last eternally because of your involvement in The 40-Day Revolution.

1. On your computer or by hand, make an "It is Finished" sticker, and then wear it!

   a. Explain to people that you are finishing the 40-day fast

   b. Explain that when Jesus died, He said, "It is finished" which means "paid in full."

   c. Explain that He paid for our sins. Finish strong, just like Jesus did.

2. Your campaign fast is completed at the end of the day. Celebrate with some friends. If you want, eat or drink whatever you've been fasting, and share stories of your experiences.

3. Your spiritual journey is just beginning! Think about and talk about how to keep the revolution alive.

4. Sit down and make a list of the things you have seen God do over the last 40 days. E-mail your testimonies to: www.operationlightforce.com

5. Ask God to help you apply what you have learned.

6. Ask God for his direction and strength regarding adjusting your lifestyle so that you can continue to bear much fruit.

SOCIAL MEDIA ASSIGNMENT - Tell the world about what God has done in your life during the last 40 days

   John 19:30 "When he had received the drink, Jesus said, 'It is finished.' With that, he bowed his head and gave up his spirit."

How has God changed my life? My youth group? My campus?

JOURNAL

What will I do to keep alive what God has started?

_____
_____
_____
_____
_____
_____
_____
_____
_____
_____
_____
_____

PRAYER

_____
_____
_____
_____
_____
_____
_____
_____
_____
_____

WEEK 6 ~ MEMORY VERSE:

II Timothy 1:13-14

"What you have heard from me, keep as the pattern of sound teaching, with faith and love in Christ Jesus. Guard the good deposit that was entrusted to you—guard it with the help of the Holy Spirit who lives in us."

[CONGRATULATIONS!]

You have just completed a **40-day assault** on the enemy's spiritual forces in your home and at school. For persevering to the end, you deserve a **"Medal of Honor."** You have become engaged in a revolution that will not stop until **Christ Jesus** returns.

KNOW THIS

You have impacted the spiritual climate of your campus, your family members, and the lives of other students in significant ways for Christ. You have made a mess of Satan's strategies, advanced Christ's kingdom, matured spiritually, and you have developed some habits that we pray will last for a lifetime.

REMEMBER

The battle is not over. Your mission has only begun. Now, your mission, should you choose to accept it, is this:

1. Love others in practical and tangible ways.

2. Serve others even as Christ served us and gave His life for us while we were still sinners.

3. Speak words of blessings to all of your friends, peers, and, yes, even your enemies.

4. Pray for the unsaved harvest. Pray for their healing, their relationship to God, and their well-being.

5. Keep on telling people about the love of God, and His gift of eternal life through Jesus' death and resurrection. Tell them how they can know God.

APPENDIX

[FORGIVENESS]

Jesus taught us **forgiveness** by His words and by His actions. In **Matthew 6,** when Jesus taught the disciples how to pray He said, *"Forgive us…as we forgive others."* It is the only part of the prayer that Jesus went on to explain to the disciples more fully.

Jesus said to His disciples that if we don't forgive others, then our heavenly Father won't forgive us. We all desperately need God's forgiveness. All of us have sinned. God wants you to be free from shame, condemnation and guilt. He sent His only Son Jesus to pay the penalty that you and I deserved to pay, so that we can be totally forgiven and cleansed.

One of the only prerequisites for being forgiven and receiving His forgiveness is to forgive others. I know that you have been hurt deeply by someone in your life. Some of you have had a life full of deep hurts, wounds, betrayal and abuse. It seems impossible to forgive those who hurt you. Their words or actions may have devastated you. For some it is your father or mother whom you loved but who walked out on you. For some it is the person who broke your trust or violated you.

It isn't easy, but it is vital for your own well-being, for your relationship with God, and for your future well being that you forgive anyone and everyone.

Let me clarify here what I am not saying.

First of all, I am not saying that if you are currently in an abusive relationship that you need to do nothing and allow the abuse to continue. If the situation warrants it, you can call the authorities, and have the person arrested. Even then, you will still need to forgive that person if you want to live a healthy life, know peace and joy in your heart.

Second, I'm not saying that you have to be best friends with those who have hurt you. You can forgive someone and maintain a healthy distance from them.

If the person who has hurt you the most is a family member and you are still around that person every day, you may need to do more than just forgive them one time. The forgiveness will be an ongoing process, and you may need to share with them many times how what they are saying or doing affects you, hurts you, and what you would prefer.

In Matthew 18, Peter asked the Lord how many times he should forgive his brother who sins against him, "7 times?" Jesus replied, no Peter, 7 times 70 times. He then told a story of a man who was forgiven a vast debt and then couldn't forgive someone who owed him. Jesus concludes that if we don't forgive others we will be tormented. Unforgiveness brings torment to our soul, our mind and to our body.

Take the time to examine your life and write down the names of everyone who has hurt you. Ask God to forgive them, ask God to help you to forgive them, then forgive that person—and do it as often as you need to.

If forgiveness is hard for you because people have hurt you deeply get more teaching on forgiveness at:

http://operationlightforce.com/100-foundational/352-jesse-s-testimony-21

[CATALOGUE]

www.40dayrevolution.com

Resources to help youth leaders carry out an effective revolution.

40-Day Revolution App

REVOLUTION OUT OF THE BOX!

If you're looking for a strategy that will help you equip your students to take their schools back for Christ . . . look no further. We understand what it takes to be a youth pastor and to work with a limited budget. That's one of the reasons we've developed Revolution Out of the Box. This exciting, new curriculum is now available!

Revolution Out of the Box contains virtually everything you need to launch a revolution! It includes: six completely prepared, powerful lessons, small group questions and handouts, video clips, Bible studies, and The 40-Day Revolution book with supply packet. Everything you need to help your students sustain a revolution for an entire six weeks!

Call Operation Light Force or go to the merchandise section on our website and check it out! Order your Revolution Out of the Box today!

- Two powerful videos to motivate, inspire, and challenge.

- Leader's Training Manual, which includes six powerful, complete lessons to help you cast the vision and train your students.

- A Supply Packet including The 40-Day Revolution book, tracts, notecards, dog tag, assignment cards.

JESUS TRAINING MANUAL

Jesus commanded His followers to "go and make disciples of all nations." This book dares you to examine how Jesus Himself made disciples.

Richard Mull's honest account of his personal journey toward biblical discipleship presents a dilemma for twenty-first-century believers: Will we adopt a system of belief that explains why we disciple differently than Jesus did, or must we admit that in spite of our education and experience, we may not be making disciples according to Jesus' teaching?

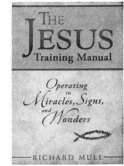

God desires to take you on a journey much like that of Jesus' first disciples, who learned to do what Jesus was doing by observing Him in action and obeying what He taught. Lord, Disciple Me will challenge you to develop a biblical foundation for your journey. Jesus will provide the hands-on experience!!

"40 DAYS TO TRANSFORMATION MANUAL"

Written for and geared toward adults, this manual will guide you on a 40-day "mission" to bring about spiritual transformation in your life, workplace, home, neighborhood, and even your city! You will learn what "transformation" really is, as well as a comprehensive understanding about what it means to fast and see God's power released through blessing, servant, and prayer evangelism.

"AGAPE REVOLUTION"

Children have been excited by what they've seen take place in their older brothers and sisters—now they can be a part, too! This manual puts simple tools into their hands that will help them change their world for Jesus. Each book contains an explanation of each of the 40 assignments, as well as quotes, scriptures, and challenges that will keep children motivated and focused during the 40 days.

"THE 40-DAY CAMPUS REVOLUTION" MANUAL

College campuses have been the starting points of most of the revolutions launched around the world—why should it be any different for this kind of "counterculture" revolution? Each manual gives a great understanding of what it means to fast and pray, the elements of the revolution, and a complete explanation about each of the 40 assignments that will be carried out over the 40 days.

ONE DAY TRAINING CONFERENCE

We will bring a one-day, four-hour training session to your city to assist you in launching "The 40-Days" with your youth group, or better yet, with your entire church family! We will focus on training and equipping each participant to understand the power of prayer, servant and blessing evangelism, and fasting.

We have seen a near 100% commitment by those who attend a ONE DAY Training to carry out the 40 days' assignments. Lives, schools, cities, neighborhoods, workplaces, and homes are radically changed for God's kingdom. Why wait? Schedule a conference and prepare to "launch a revolution" today!

LORD HEAL ME

"Lord, Heal Me" Traces the biblical foundation of healing from Genesis to Revelation. There are many testimonies of God healing the sick today. You will grow in faith and in understanding of what the bible teaches about this very important subject. This is a must for every follower of Jesus who wants to be like Jesus, do what Jesus did and teach what Jesus taught.

GOD SPEAKS BIBLE

An amazing Bible that will help you to live the supernatural life. It will impact Bible reading for a new generation. This Bible highlights every time that God speaks throughout the Bible. It also highlights every miracle and every dream, vision and encounter with angels.

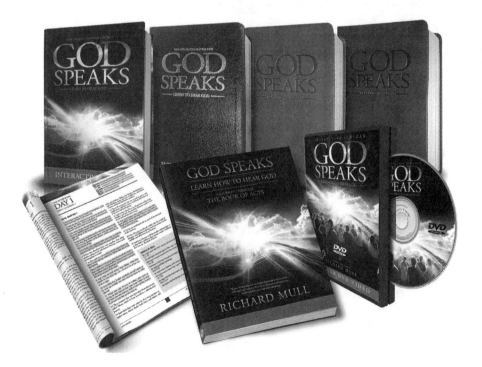

OPERATION LIGHT FORCE
2310 Leonard Drive | Seffner, FL 33584
www.operationlightforce.com
www.40dayrevolution.com
813.657.6147 phone